W9-AAR-300

You've thought about it, dreamed about it, talked about it . . .

So why aren't you married?

Are you already spoken for—
by parents who don't want to let go?

Have you scared potential mates away?

Are you a late bloomer?

Do you try too hard?

Do you pick doomed relationships?

Are you setting impossible standards?

In this wise and witty guide, leading relationship expert Sharyn Wolf tells you what to do to get to the altar. Complete with personal stories and self-help tests that pinpoint the factors in your life that are holding you back, *So You Want to Get Married* reveals all you need to know to turn a date into a mate, including The Most Important Things You Will Ever Learn About a Great Marriage.

Soon you'll be naming the date and
planning your wedding!

Sharyn Wolf, C.S.W., is a psychotherapist, marriage counselor, and online advice columnist. She has appeared on numerous television shows, including *48 Hours, Today,* and *Oprah.* She is the author of *Guerrilla Dating Tactics* and *How to Stay Lovers for Life,* both available from Plume. She and her husband live in New York City.

Also by Sharyn Wolf

50 Ways to Find a Lover
Guerrilla Dating Tactics
How to Stay Lovers for Life

So You Want to Get

Married

Guerrilla Tactics for
Turning a Date into a Mate

Sharyn Wolf

A PLUME BOOK

APR 0 5 2000

PLUME
Published by the Penguin Group
Penguin Putnam Inc., 375 Hudson Street, New York, New York 10014, U.S.A.
Penguin Books Ltd, 27 Wrights Lane, London W8 5TZ, England
Penguin Books Australia Ltd, Ringwood, Victoria, Australia
Penguin Books Canada Ltd, 10 Alcorn Avenue, Toronto, Ontario, Canada M4V 3B2
Penguin Books (N.Z.) Ltd, 182–190 Wairau Road, Auckland 10, New Zealand

Penguin Books Ltd, Registered Offices: Harmondsworth, Middlesex, England

First published by Plume, a member of Penguin Putnam Inc.

First Printing, June, 1999
10 9 8 7 6 5 4 3 2 1

Copyright © Sharyn Wolf, 1999
All rights reserved

 REGISTERED TRADEMARK—MARCA REGISTRADA

LIBRARY OF CONGRESS CATALOGING-IN-PUBLICATION DATA
Wolf, Sharyn.
    So you want to get married : guerilla tactics for turning a date into a mate / Sharyn Wolf.
        p.   cm.
    ISBN 0-452-28012-5
    1. Mate selection.   2. Dating (Social customs).   3. Man-woman relationships.   I. Title.
HQ801.W795   1999
646.7'7—dc21   98-49651
                                                                                 CIP

Printed in the United States of America
Set in Palatino
Designed by Leonard Telesca

Without limiting the rights under copyright reserved above, no part of this publication
may be reproduced, stored in or introduced into a retrieval system, or transmitted, in any
form, or by any means (electronic, mechanical, photocopying, recording, or otherwise),
without the prior written permission of both the copyright owner and the above
publisher of this book.

BOOKS ARE AVAILABLE AT QUANTITY DISCOUNTS WHEN USED TO PROMOTE PRODUCTS OR
SERVICES. FOR INFORMATION PLEASE WRITE TO PREMIUM MARKETING DIVISION, PENGUIN
PUTNAM INC., 375 HUDSON STREET, NEW YORK, NEW YORK 10014.

I dedicate this book to my smart, adorable friend, who has no trouble getting dates, but she doesn't want any more dates. She wants to get married. I don't have to tell you her name.

At this point, she's pretty frustrated. She's had three relationships that fizzled out. Her best friend just got married, as did her secretary, her dentist, and her exterminator. She has bruises from all the diamond rings that are getting poked in her face and from being recklessly hugged by the blissful couples.

My adorable friend is more adorable than any of them. And smarter. And more interesting. In fact, she's a damn good catch for any man. The question she keeps asking herself is: *Why not me?*

I have the answer to that. I plan to spend my first huge royalty check on her wedding gift.

Acknowledgments

Deb Brody is my editor, my friend, and my lunch and gossip pal. I may do the writing, but her talent is my best asset. Thank you, Deb.

My clients are my teachers and my wise allies. Thank you.

Contents

III. *Postcommitment Stress Disorder*

IV. *So You're Going to Get Married*

Introduction

Terry and Kyle have dated for ages. Everything is great, except for the fact that Kyle hasn't proposed. Terry wants to marry him, but how long should she wait? Should she be the one to propose first? Should she just keep hinting? Or does Kyle know something she doesn't know?

Nancy likes Larry, but he wants to "keep it light." This isn't the first time this has happened to her. Does she have some secret gene that generates a commitophobe-attraction scent?

Peter is wild about Ellen . . . er . . . except he thinks she wears cheap shoes. He loves the way she makes him feel . . . but . . . that bad haircut. It's easy to give his heart to her . . . except . . . these little details of her inferior style of dress hold him back. If she'd take care more about her clothes and her hair, he'd marry her . . . of course . . . then . . . there's the issue of her unmanicured nails.

Royce hasn't had a date in years. Should he let that stop him from setting a wedding date?

This book is for those of you who know that you want to get married but you're not the type to play farcical games in the attempt to snag a mate. This book will not help you if what you want is casual romance. It will not help you cruise all the eligible people in your zip code. It has one purpose: *To help you get or make a proposal.* It will explain the key to a deep, loving attachment that will have him thinking that nothing is as much fun without you as it is with you; that will have her missing you in the time it takes to walk to her bus stop; that will evoke in him the urgent need to hold you in his arms again.

You don't even have to have a certain someone in mind, although if you do, that's great. If the two of you seem just right for each other, even better. And, as can be the case, if the two of you are just right for each other, but he hasn't realized it yet, you are definitely holding the right pages in your hand.

Lastly, if you want to get married but you are presently partnerless, relax. You will be so waggishly appealing by the time you finish reading that that man will think he won the lottery in meeting you; that woman won't be able to get you off her mind.

Let's not waste time. You've probably done too much of that already.

PART 1

The First Four Steps Down the Aisle

The First Step
Down the Aisle

Symmetry

I know what it takes to get someone to fall in love with you in a way that will make him want to marry you, need to marry you, to make his life complete. I know what it takes to make her long for you, to doodle your names as Mr. and Mrs. It isn't sex or money or a big red Porsche. The key to the aisle is in understanding the nature of attachment. He must be thinking about you when he spots a couple kissing on the street. She must start to accidentally call people by your name. He must be sure that nothing is as much fun without you as it is with you. She must start to think more highly of Ding Dongs simply because you love Ding Dongs.

 Put ten people together in a room with hammers. After twenty minutes, they will all hammer in a certain rhythm.

You have control over three main components of the type of attachment that leads to marriage, the three things that separate the soon-to-be-marrieds from the I-can't-find-anybody's. They are symmetry, empathy, and disclosure, and all three will be explained in the following chapters. Without them you can have wonderful dates that end up going nowhere and you'll never know why. So you start to think it's you. And you already know where that leads.

When you understand symmetry, empathy, and disclosure it won't mean love at first sight (she has to be able to warm up to your face, your scent, your hound, Rufus), but you will know exactly how to take a tiny spark and fan it into the red hot flame of love, and then you will know how to turn love into marriage. Your confidence will soar—and nothing is more marriageable than confidence and style.

Make Him Want You

When the more you talk, the more you find to talk about—well, that's symmetry. Two minds, one freeway, same direction. Early symmetry occurs when two people find out that they have things in common. You don't need to have everything in common—just enough to keep you talking. Sure, this sounds old hat. However, *it's not shared interests that make symmetry matter.* Symmetry matters because people *attribute meaning* to it. Symmetry creates the easy feeling that you two, out of all others on the earth, met because you were meant to meet; you were meant to be together.

 Symmetrical Replies
You love Abba? I love Abba.
No kidding. I thought I was the only one who still drank Nestle's.
I'm a Democrat, too.

Nonsymmetrical Replies
Abba? Is that the band where the girls play the instruments?
Don't you watch your cholesterol?
I'm not into politics.

Symmetry makes a chance rendezvous feel like fate.

This is what you need to cultivate if you want him to want you.

How to Cultivate the Feeling That This Was Meant to Be

Sure, he can think you're cute, but you're still going to have to say something. The following will help you to pique his curiosity so his interest will travel beyond your symmetrical bosom and into your symmetrical heart.

1. Go on a maniacal symmetry search.

When there is a spark, begin a symmetry search for something you share. Oh, not the obvious things that everybody likes, but the obscure things, the uncommon things, the "secret" things that make the two of you feel that you are sharing a delicious moment that you couldn't share with anyone else. *Keep talking* until you discover that you both

have pierced navels

have your teeth cleaned regularly *only* because you both love the nitrous oxide

sleep until 3:00 P.M. on Sundays

think Brad Pitt should wash his hair more often

love Samuel Fuller's movies

would never admit how much you love Michael Bolton

have deviated septums

are ticklish behind the knees

Couples have cemented a relationship because during childhood, they both once dressed as a ghost on Halloween, or because each once had a friend named Nancy, or they both lost a toy train on a real train.

What complementary quirks can you locate and make meaningful? What coincidences can you uncover that might not be coincidences at all?

2. Accept an offer or make a counteroffer.

Think of everything he says, the topics he brings up, even offhand remarks, as an offering—a gift he is giving you as Caesar gave gifts to Cleopatra. Then, use the topics he brings up as part of your symmetry search, even if the meaning is not immediately apparent.

Simple

You are out having dinner when a foreign woman tries to enter the restaurant with her dog and is told that dogs aren't allowed in restaurants.

He says: I lived in France for two years, and I could take my dog in most restaurants.

Say: Well, let's fly to Paris next time we have lunch, so your dog can come, too.

Don't say: Uggggh, I can't imagine it.

More Complicated

You don't follow politics, and you're lucky if you remember who is running for what. You are on a bus when the guy next to you starts talking to you.

He says: What do you think of the Republican convention?

Say: I haven't kept up, but I bet you have. What's your take? Then I won't have to listen to all those boring speeches.

Don't say: I'm apolitical.

Even More Complicated

You are at a party. You have just begun to talk to a nice woman. Who knows? You might really click. The first few minutes are fine.

> She says: It's noisy. Let's get out of here and go someplace quieter. Do you live near here?

> Say: It looks quieter in that corner over there. Let's walk there and keep talking.

> Don't say: No way, fresh girl.

 When one person yawns, everybody yawns.

Find something in the conversation worth responding to. Don't confuse accepting the offer as meaning you have to do what he wants or act the way you think she wants you to act. You can always make a counteroffer. But don't reject the offer and close her out, even if her offer feels a little off to you.

> REMEMBER: You don't have to agree or even go along. You can always make a counteroffer, but accepting the offer is a way to create a sense of symmetry, a shared moment that's meant for just the two of you.

3. Leave him wanting more.

Betty and Lionel couldn't remember the last time they'd each actually laughed out loud on a first date. Dinner was so much fun that they decided to go for a nightcap at Rocco's Cafe. The nightcap was so much fun they decided to go for cappuccino at Felicia's Diner. Cappuccino was so much fun that they decided to go to Betty's and listen to her Coltrane CDs. From the moment they walked through her doorway, a little voice told Betty that they were going to end up you-know-where. But by three A.M., they were exhausted, neither could sleep, and embarrassment had planted itself between them. In the following weeks, they made a few halfhearted attempts to recapture their enthusiasm, but things seemed to fizzle out.

When you love someone, you can sit at a Sunday brunch with the newspaper, never say or hear a word, and think, "Oh, these are our quiet times together. How nice." But, if this happened during an early encounter with your future wife, you'd freak out. Silence increases as intimacy increases. Early silences are tougher for many people to tolerate. So when you are together in the early part of your romance, there tends to be less silence. Therefore, you need to know when you are sapped. It's great to throw caution to the wind every once in a while and go on an early date that lasts from Sunday until Tuesday, but in general, it makes more sense to know when that interesting talk you've had together has begun to devolve into

everything you never wanted to know about his ex

everything you shouldn't be saying about yours

l-o-n-g l-u-l-l-s

sex you won't feel great about when you wake up tomorrow

You can always get together again soon, but, like the Catskill comedians know, it's best to leave them wanting more.

4. Remember: Your body speaks volumes.

Early on, in addition to your awareness of what the two of you have to talk about, pay just as much attention to how the two of you use touch, personal space, and other aspects of body language. After all, messages, both exciting and disturbing, can be transmitted through touch without a word being spoken.

The use of touch:

Jerry was knocked out by Eileen, and she felt the same way about him—until the day early on in their relationship when he took to giving her a shoulder massage while they were watching a concert. She felt absolutely invaded and had to fight the impulse to get up and leave. Her family had always kept loving displays a private matter. Jerry would never have known, because his last girlfriend, Sarah, offered *him* a shoulder massage on their first date.

Culturally, we all have different ideas about how much touch is appropriate early on. One woman runs her finger across his shoulder, whereas another woman sees this as a highly sexualized gesture. Observe how the person you are with uses touch and keep within his or her boundaries. You may reach out and touch someone lightly on the wrist, but then note the reaction to your touch. Does she smile? Pull her wrist back? Touch you? Look off into the distance? Fidget? If she appears uncomfortable, do not continue to touch her. In fact, *don't invade her critical distance.*

The sense of personal space:

My husband, who is a musician, had several concerts that took him from New York City to Tokyo. He and the members of The Ron Carter Quintet, for whom he plays bass, were astonished as they walked down the street and found that people bumped into them right and left as if it were nothing. The guys in the band originally greeted the bumps as personal affronts and responded like New York City taxi drivers. They soon realized that *they* were the foreigners.

 Many a person has dumped someone after a first date simply because the date presumed to sit too close to her too soon.

In Tokyo, the crowds bump into each other without a second thought. In New York City, you'd better be careful not to bump, no matter how Olympian your attempt to squeeze by must be. In relationships such differences can make love bloom or fizzle fast. You must make an assessment of your partner's sense of personal space. Is he taking a step closer to you? When you step in, do his eyes dart around the room? Make sure you leave adequate personal space early on, even if you can't get as close to him as you'd like. Once he knows you better, then you can move in for the kill.

Your body movements:

Do you move like the funky chicken is playing in your head, while she moves like a Beethoven sonata is playing in hers? Without perfecting the old Harpo-sees-himself-in-the-mirror routine, be aware of how you each use your body. Does he lean up against a wall (he's shy talking to you and the wall is giving him support)? Does she put her legs up on the table (she's letting you know she's alpha)? Does he unscrew the tops off the salt and pepper shakers and the ketchup (he's underage, even if he's thirty-five)? Think about what her body language is conveying to you. Look, I'm sure you've noticed her body! Noticing her body language may help you reevaluate what you were about to do next.

 Symmetry builds harmony, increases curiosity, and demonstrates a genuine interest in what the other person enjoys.

---

5. Be a good fit.

When couples achieve a good fit, they don't feel antagonized or stuck with a relationship they don't enjoy. They feel unobstructed to express themselves in their own way, and neither feels bothered by the partner's behavior, even if the behavior would seem peculiar to others. For example:

Good fit: Marcella is the type of person who worries about what will happen ten years from now. She is likely to pop up in bed in the middle of the night and quip, "Oh my God, have I put enough money into my IRA?" Marcella's quirks amuse her boyfriend, Lester, to no end, providing him with endless stories to tell his friends.

Bad fit: Marcella worries about what will happen ten years from now. She is likely to pop up in bed at four A.M. and say to her boyfriend, Lester, "Oh my God, am I putting enough into my IRA?" Lester, sufferer of a long-term sleep disorder . . .

Good fit: Carmen talks baby talk when she and Jorge are alone. Jorge, who came from a family where there was only animosity between his parents never had the chance to be a happy baby. Carmen's style feels healing, comforting, charming to Jorge.

Bad fit: Carmen talks baby talk when she and Jorge are alone. Jorge gets a new job that totally stresses him out. He needs to talk to Carmen about his burden and whether he should leave his job. Carmen gives a goofy grin, and says, "Hewwo-o-o HoHay." Jorge realizes that he will *always* be the parent, even when he *needs* to have a wife.

Above all, more than anything that you both love or both hate, more than anything that you share together, more than any sexual eccentricity that turns you both on, it matters to be a good fit.

REMEMBER: Being a good fit never means you agree with everything she says or you always want to go to the same restaurant she does. That is not being a good fit; that is being a doormat.

Good fits depend on what you have in common, *and* what you have that is different but complements each other. Good fits pinch-hit for each other's temporary lapses—they take over, instruct, or bail each other out when necessary. Good fits can be practical, such as his love of baking and her love of warm cookies or her love of dark meat and his love of white meat.

Good fits must also be emotional:

Terry had gone with Andrew—her then boyfriend, now husband—into a restaurant. They had only been seeing each other a short time, so she was still on best behavior. Two minutes after they left she realized she'd left her favorite scarf on the back of her chair. For reasons she could not fathom, she was scared to call the restaurant and ask them if her scarf was there. She entreated Andrew to call for her. He thought she was being silly about this—it was so unlike her, he said. He wanted to interrogate her about her behavior, yet he could see how important it was to her. So, he asked no questions, and he did it. Terry recounts it as a pivotal moment. Andrew's acceptance of her quirky behavior made him an emotionally good fit for Terry.

By the way, true good fits have reciprocity. Terry has had more than her share of stepping in for Andrew. When two people have a good fit, the relationship is the safest place in the world.

 My mother first met my stepfather in junior high school and he was her date to the prom. However, she married my dad, and he died twenty years later. My stepfather had been a family friend and he had remained single. He always said he'd get married if he met someone like my mom. He was a pallbearer at my father's funeral. Two years later he married my mother.

Symmetry Mistake

The big mistake made in the name of symmetry is when you think that lots of symmetry automatically means the two of you will fall in love.

Evan and Deidre had more compatible likes and dislikes than seemed possible. Obscure poets, postwar German writers, bebop, merlot. They read each other's poems while listening to Charlie Parker in Sweden. It took Evan three months to figure out that Deidre didn't value their similarities in the way he did. She was not going to fall in love with him. He had refused to believe it because they were so compatible. But though their symmetry was everything symmetry could be, it was the *only* thing they had. Deidre loved having so much in common with Evan, but he just wasn't her type and she couldn't get past that.

Next time you are sitting across from someone you have a high symmetry quotient with, and a little voice in your head keeps whispering, "What's wrong with this picture?" listen to the little voice. Symmetry alone will not make a marriage. The next two chapters will describe the other two components of love that must be present in order for a deep attachment to form.

 My husband felt that the two of us were meant to marry because his older brother, who had passed away, was born during the same month and the same year that I was born. Moreover, when his brother died, the book on his night table was a Tom Robbins book that featured a tribe of red-haired people, and I had red hair.

6. If none of this makes sense for you, ignore it.

Remember that symmetry is the skeleton of a relationship, a structure to hang the relationship on. So, if you still haven't found anything in common, but you think you'd have fun anyway, *go for it!* In fact, suggest that you try something fun together—wade in a pond, take up bowling, play "Chopsticks," make a root beer float. Pretend you never read this chapter and fall in love anyway.

 Marisol walked down the street under a cloud of depression. A man passed her and said, "You look so sad." She snapped, "I am, but why should you care?" He replied, "I do care." They started talking, and got married three months later.

Symmetry

1. Go on a maniacal symmetry search.
2. Accept an offer or make a counteroffer.
3. Leave him wanting more.
4. Remember: Your body speaks volumes.
5. Be a good fit.
6. If you still haven't found anything in common, but you think you'd have fun anyway, *go for it!* You'll take up something new together. In fact, suggest that you try something new together—wade in a pond, take up the clarinet, make sushi.

2

The Second Step
Down the Aisle

Empathy

At any time my office telephone may ring, and I will be greeted by a person—let's call her Mary—who was referred to me for psychotherapy. I don't know Mary or her problem, or the nuances of her character, her coping skills, or her personal history. Usually we set up an initial consultation, both of us hoping that I can understand and help.

When we first meet, there will be awkwardness. We have to get used to each other's faces, conversational styles, twitches, the way we sit, the amount of eye contact we make or don't make. I try to ask the right questions and to carefully listen to the answers. I look for what is said, what is inferred, and what is not said. Most important, while I am aware of all of my thoughts and feelings, I listen with a clean mind. I do not dwell on how I might feel if I were in Mary's shoes. This moment is not about how I might feel. My job is to tune my mental radio dial to Mary's channel—to feel along with her as she is feeling.

 Symmetry is facts of the mind.
Empathy is facts of the body.

I never cease to be amazed at psychotherapists who offer the initial consultation for free. What are they thinking? A first visit is by far the most challenging, and I'm tempted to charge twice as much. I will *never* work harder for this person—there will never be more on the line for me. If I understand her and I can articulate it in a way that jibes with her experience, I will have a new client. If I misread her, wander off on the wrong tangent, offer bad advice, come across as judgmental, act shocked by what she says, appear to be a twitty know-it-all, focus only on the obvious, seem clueless, say too much or too little, fail to pick up on an important cue . . . well, she will leave me and find someone else. I want a client, she wants a therapist.

Expectations run high as we tentatively dance our first dance. I have one goal in the first psychotherapy session. Our future together hinges on it: *Can I help this person to feel safe with me?*

If she doesn't feel safe, she won't tell me what is really on her mind, and she will not think she is in the right place after all. If she doesn't feel safe, she will not believe that I can understand, and nothing between us can work.

On the other hand, if she does feel safe, her guard will come down, and she will look for what is right with what I say rather than what is wrong with it. She will reveal the heart of the matter, and she will consider the possibility that, in time, she can trust me.

Empathy Makes the Relationship a Safe Place to Be

This ability to create a safe place for another person to think and feel and talk is called empathy. It is the second step toward marriage. You don't need to be perfect at empathy or even to feel empathic most of the time, you just need to be *good enough* at it to move the relationship forward. Here are some of the many ways that empathy has been described:

- your ability to understand and respond to the inner life of another
- your ability to read your partner with an intuition that goes beyond what he says or does

---

 Symmetry is curiosity about interests.
Empathy is curiosity about feelings.

- your motivation to visit another person's internal land-scape—the place within that holds deepest joys and wildest feelings and, sometimes, unspeakable desires
- your capacity for deep connections with others
- your intelligence that moves you in ways that surprise you
- your ability to tune in to how others truly react in your presence and to know about the impact you have on the world
- learning to hold another's feelings as gently as a mother holds a baby
- rapport
- intuition
- altruism
- accuracy in personal perception
- ability to accurately receive another's feelings

 Milly told me about a meeting of professionals
she went to where everyone was very smart and
verbal and thoughtful and mindful . . . but
everyone was so intent on making thoughtful
points, that nobody listened to anyone else. Lots
of brains don't make empathy happen.

The good news is that empathy is already biologically engineered into your genes. You were born with the capacity for intimate exchange, so don't worry that you have to learn something new. From the moment your mother looked in your eyes and you looked back and the two of you connected with no need to speak, you were an empathy impresario. The reason empathy seems complicated is that, like love, it is mysterious and delicious and defies easy explanations. As the great psychiatrist Harry Stack Sullivan pointed out, empathy does not refer to what you see, what you hear, or any other sense receptor. Empathy is not in sound waves or air waves—and it's okay to let it be mysterious because so much in life *is* mysterious.

> NOTE: Do not go out and practice empathy without reading the next chapter on disclosure.

Empathy Comes with Deep Listening

All you have to do to make a safe, empathic space is:

ListenListenListenListenListenListenListenListenListen
    ListenListenListenListen

Think about it. We spend our lives looking for someone who will really listen. In fact, that's how I stay in business. Even the smallest evidence that we haven't been heard—such as an unreturned phone call or an unanswered email or when someone you know passes by without a proper hello—can leave a person feeling hurt, bitter, or confused and can make a person retreat from closeness. We can be great listeners. When you ask your best friend how she is and she says fine and you know she's not, how do you know? You know because you listen beyond her words. Since you have history together, you have a basis for comparison with her past behavior. Because you know her, you are equipped to take a seismic reading of her emotional life. Because you are motivated to listen to her, you really listen as she has really listened to you. Friendship is based largely on deep listening.

Symmetry is gathering concrete information.
Empathy is gathering abstract information.

However, most of us are much worse listeners than we think we are. We hear what we want to hear, what we dread hearing, what we think we should hear, and what we think we shouldn't. Often, what we hear has little to do with what was said. One expert said that ninety-five percent of what we hear has to do with us (our needs, values) and only five percent has to do with what the person is saying. The worst part of this pathetic statistic is that it's probably accurate.

So, clear your mind of your own agenda, and take this time to upgrade your emotional decoding skills.

 Empathic listening transforms relationships because people yearn and long to be heard.

Emotional Decoding Skills

1. Step out of your head and into his.

In order to cultivate empathy, most of the talking time must be spent with an interpersonal focus rather than an introspective one.

Introspective is you thinking about you.
Interpersonal is you interacting with him.

Get introspective when you go home. It's best, when you are dating with marriage in mind, to pay attention to what he says and how he feels and how he reacts to what you say, and how that makes you feel. Pay attention to his facial expressions

expressive gestures

vocal intonation

slouching shoulders

pace of speech

energy level

Notice when his expressions match his words and when they don't.

2. Validate his feelings even if you don't agree with them.

During deep listening, don't jump in with a competing opinion, even if you have one. This is the time to *listen and learn more* about this person. Gather information. Encourage him to say more with statements such as:

I see what you are saying . . .
You seem to feel passionate about this . . .

3. Let him know he can count on you for understanding.

It can be fun to finish each other's thoughts if that's your relationship style, but, for now, gather his thoughts, his view of the world, his inner life.

Don't interrupt.
Don't offer advice, even if it's good advice.
Don't jump to agree or disagree, even if you have strong feelings.

4. Cultivate your sensitivity.

"You sound worried. Are you?"
"Ooooh, that's a scary story. Were you scared?"

It's always worthwhile to check with her about what she is feeling. Never assume she feels the same way you do, even if it seems obvious to you. Instead, notice how she appears to be feeling and then ask to find out if you are correct.

5. Remain accepting of different conversational styles, pacing, pausing.

Respect those who requires some quiet—let them sort their thoughts through without chomping at the bit to pipe in.

 Don't just do something: *stand there!*

Respect the person who wants to talk things through. Even if "it's really nothing" for you, he may need to spell it all out.

6. Practice patience.

Even if you can't wait to say something, when your mind starts jumping around, slow it down with conscious effort.

7. Ask her how her day was.

Many people nod their heads without hearing a word you say. They pretend to be interested. They ask questions and then fidget while you try to answer, or worse, they stare into space or at their watch or at the Pamela Anderson lookalike who just walked through the door. But not you!! Show that you are motivated to get to know her. Maybe she had a rough day and that's why she wants to end the date early. Maybe her dog is sick. Don't jump to conclusions. Find out what her experience has been with the world that day.

- Listen for feelings, but don't push for feelings.
- Welcome feedback, but don't fish for feedback.
- Strive for empathic accuracy even if you can't achieve it.

8. Get out of the way.

I did a radio show in Denver, and a man called in to tell me that he wanted to do something special for a woman he was in love with for Valentine's Day. He said that he'd been very thoughtful, but all his attempts to win her love had failed. I asked him to tell me one thing he'd done. He said that he'd called her answering machine and played all his favorite oldies for her. Well, his heart was in the right place, but his empathy was not. He was doing something for her that he would have wanted done for himself. He didn't have a clue about what she might want for herself.

Sometimes we make the mistake of trying to use our relationships to bolster ourselves, meet our own needs, look good in someone else's eyes, have them reflect ourselves back to us in a positive fashion. All this is okay, but, early on, it will be much more productive to get out of the way and learn to listen to what he really wants or needs from you. Make room for someone besides yourself to love.

9. Anticipate ambivalence so you won't be thrown by it.

When and where a relationship makes the glorious shift into love is uncertain, but one thing is for sure: Time will change how you see each other. So don't be surprised when you pick up on his alternating thoughts about you. During any given evening, he may think:

- You are the one I've been waiting for.
- You are so competent you'd never want me.
- Well, if you don't want me maybe I don't want you.
- Why did I ever go out with you anyway, you're not really special.
- Then, again . . .

 Ancient Hebrew law required a man to marry his deceased brother's widow.

He will have all kinds of feelings about you—sometimes simultaneously. No, he's not a psycho, he's smart, and smart people play out multiple scenarios as they try on ideas. Because you're smart too, not to mention empathic, you may sense his ambivalence. Anticipate it. Expect it. And, don't let it overwhelm you in the beginning. *Your ability to tolerate his initial shifts in feeling toward you will be a key part of your ability to win him over.*

10. Consider this an exercise in spring training for your heart.

In teaching psychotherapists how to help their clients, the pioneering psychiatrist Karen Horney said that you can only go as far with your clients as you have gone with yourself. The same thing holds true for your relationship. You can only go as far with your relationship as you have gone with yourself.

You see, the key to marriage and true love lies in knowing that it does not begin with *finding* the right person, it begins with *being* the right person. Even if you've had your heart broken many times, empathic listening will lead you toward marriage because it is a building block of intimacy. Using it properly will make you more lovable than you've ever realized because it will build your confidence, show that you are to be taken seriously, and fortify you for a serious love.

Think of it this way: Even the oldest, most tired, and worst injured player can go through spring training, bounce back, and surprise the nation. You could end up surprising the nation, but, more to the point, it's time to surprise yourself.

Empathy

1. Step out of your head and into his.
2. Validate his feelings even if you don't agree with them.
3. Let him know he can count on you for understanding.
4. Cultivate your sensitivity.
5. Remain accepting of different conversational styles, pacing, pausing.
6. Practice patience.
7. Ask her how her day was.
8. Get out of the way.
9. Anticipate ambivalence so you won't be thrown by it.
10. Consider this an exercise in spring training for your heart.

 Dot lived in New York City and her fiancé lived in Denver. Because they both had good jobs, it was hard to decide who should move. Dot decided to take a four-month leave of absence from her job, and try out Denver. Her office replaced her. The night before she was leaving her fiancé called the whole thing off, stating that it was too much responsibility. Imagine how she felt as she called her office and asked if there was another job she could do. She was told that her job was big enough that two people could do it if she was willing to share an office with her replacement. She agreed, came to work the next day, and met her replacement, Kyle. Dot ended up marrying the guy hired to replace her.

First Assessment: Is It Enough?

He floats your boat. You're bursting with hope and uncertainty and hormonal tidal waves. But you've been here before. Is he someone you should run *to* or run *from*? Take this quiz to know more.

> REMEMBER: S/he doesn't have to be perfect, and neither do you. Just perfect enough.

Circle One

My heart thumps enough.

True   *Pretty Much*   *False*

We sustain decent-enough conversations.

True   *Pretty Much*   *False*

I'm having enough fun.

True   *Pretty Much*   *False*

We're culturally simpatico enough.

True   *Pretty Much*   *False*

S/he listens and gives relevant-enough feedback.

True   *Pretty Much*   *False*

S/he is consistent enough.

True   *Pretty Much*   *False*

I could imagine often enough continuing this relationship for another seventy years.

True   Pretty Much   False

S/he has no major outstanding felony charges against her/him.

True   False   The charges were dropped

I did not meet her by taking her name off the men's room wall.

True   False   It's okay because she's the one who put her name there

DailyDoubleDailyDoubleDailyDoubleDailyDouble

We laugh enough.

True   Pretty Much   False

Scale

Ten *True:*   Call the rabbi.

Mixed between *True* and *Pretty Much:*   You're right where you should be—in an exploratory phase.

Up to three *False:*   Proceed with caution.

More than three *False:*   Calling all therapists. We've got a live one here!

> **NOTE:** If you answered *False* to the Daily Double, that counts double.

Congratulations

You've decided to move forward. That's great. Because, otherwise, you know what will happen. You have X number of dates. He shows you his. You show him yours. It goes on and on and on . . . *without ever getting serious.*

I mean, how many times have you, after weeks of what you thought were great times, shuddered when he told you that he wants to "keep it light"? Weeks later you still don't know if there was any clue, something you didn't notice that would have told you that this wouldn't work. When you understand the simple concept of the next chapter on disclosure you'll almost always know whether your partner wants to move forward. In fact, I think it's the most important chapter in this book because it clarifies the key for turning your relationship into marriage. It is also the chapter that will help you determine whether you have landed a marriageable mook or an unmarriageable mook. It will tell you exactly what to say, how and when to say it, and whether you will be able to gauge your partner's reactions to you and the relationship.

You see, you can have symmetry with anyone, friend or foe. You can have empathy with a forlorn kid in a soup commercial. But disclosures, that is the stuff that good marriages are made of.

CHAPTER 3

The Third Step Down the Aisle

Disclosure

Al notices Brianna looking off into space. He's sure he's boring her. Meanwhile, Brianna is actually trying not to stare at Al because she's afraid he will notice she's nervous. She's nervous because she likes him so much. He's nervous because he can't seem to find a topic that engages her. How can two people who like each other so-o-o much be so misguided in their interpretations of what the other is thinking?

Natalie might get fired. She can't seem to click with her new boss. When she meets Dave for dinner, she decides not to mention it because why should he be burdened? Dave can see that Natalie is preoccupied. "Of course, of course," he thinks. "She's going to blow me off." He becomes a bit defensive, and the whole night is a bust.

Connie invites Ray to come to her beach house for the weekend. Ray jumps at the chance, but when he gets there he realizes that Connie is much better off financially than he is. He is sure when she finds that out she will no longer be as interested. Connie notices Ray is less talkative. She decides that he wasn't as interested in an intimate relationship as he seemed to be. She feels rejected. He feels ashamed. Neither knows what went wrong.

It's pretty easy to know when he's troubled. His facial expressions and his body language speak volumes, even when he doesn't. But it's nearly impossible to know what he's troubled about. You can guess, but a guess is all it is. You can't be sure about the specific thing that upset him, and just as you can't know what he's troubled about, he's unlikely to know the impact of his distress on you. That is where disclosure comes in.

A disclosure is a snapshot of your inner life. It is your personal landscape of thoughts, feelings, fantasies, life events. It is the you that only your intimate partner will know—when you are ready to share it. A disclosure is an "I" statement that paints a picture. Since it is your personal inner experience, it is never a "you" statement, never a blaming statement.

 This guy . . . he listens. The more he listens, the more you want to say. But how much should you tell him, and when? Does he need to know about Franco? Or Darrin? Or Sven? Does he need to know that, on a dare, you shoplifted a can of chicken noodle soup when you were in college? That your ex cheated on you, and that you want to get married and have two children and trade in your Toyota for a Mercury Sable station wagon?

And that you think you're falling in love with him, when do you say that?

A disclosure is a way to display generosity in your relationship because it is a statement of your ability to reveal your true self; in other words, it shows trust. It is not always easy to know what you are feeling and why you are feeling that way, and it is certainly not always easy to share it. It is especially difficult to trust. In any marriage-bound relationship, knowing what you feel and why you feel that way and trusting your partner to hear it—well, it's a worthy goal.

Low-Risk Disclosures

Some disclosures are low-risk. The disclosures you make to the stranger behind you in a supermarket checkout line will almost always be low-risk.

I shouldn't eat this high-fat ice cream, but I had the urge to treat myself.
I hate these lines. I want to scream.

With a partner, a low-risk disclosure reveals a small part of you that has minimal impact on her. It's not the kind of thing that should set her off—although, you can never predict the reactions of another. You share her troubles, hopes, and your general experience of *yourself* as an individual:

Say this: I wish *I* were shorter.

Not this: I wish *you* were taller.

Say this: I'm not a fan of horror movies.

Not this: You're not going to tell me you actually enjoyed that?

Say this: I have mixed feelings about my breast enlargement.

Not this: You liked my old ones better. *Go ahead—say it!*

Disclosures Take Place in Time Zones

Disclosures can be personal facts that your partner may or may not know about you. Somehow you feel that until you've expressed your thoughts out loud, she doesn't really know you. You want her to know because you want to move the relationship forward. Telling her and watching her reaction will help you gauge how important you are in her life, and whether she's *really* interested in getting closer.

You can say more or you can say less. In other words, you can decide how much of yourself you want to part with. You can monitor the intensity, depending on whether your disclosures reflect your past, your present, or your future. Yes, disclosure can encompass three time zones. This happens when you reveal yourself, and then go on to tell your feelings about what you've revealed.

Revealing yourself: I'm part Native American and part Scottish.

Feelings about the past: When I was younger kids teased me and called me names because I looked different. That was hard on me.

Feelings about the present: I've wondered if my heritage concerns you because you're Italian.

Feelings about the future: One day, if we had children . . .

Revealing yourself: I've dated lots of men.

Feelings about the past: I used to think something was wrong with me because nothing clicked.

Feelings about the present: Since I met you, I know that it was worth the wait.

Feelings about the future: I think I've finally come to understand that phrase "the best is yet to come."

Revealing yourself: I'm sixty-two.

Feelings about the past: Once I never thought I'd live to be this age.

Feelings about the present: Now that I've met you, I feel like a kid again.

Feelings about the future: And, next year, I want to be the one to throw you your twenty-second birthday party, darling.

High-Risk Disclosures

You can see how disclosures can be low-risk or high-risk. High-risk disclosures reveal the heart of your internal landscapes. They reveal *your experience of yourself within the context of your relationship*. What you say will have a direct impact on your partner. Rule one of a high-risk disclosure (as with all disclosures) is that it should never place blame. A disclosure provides a hidden opportunity to get closer to her rather than to push her away. Again, the disclosure needs to be clearly framed in "I"s:

Say this: I get scared so I hold back.

Not this: You make me afraid to talk.

Say this: I feel alone.

Not this: You're not there for me.

Or, while raising the subject of marriage:

What you said: You never bring up marriage.

What you could have said: I've been thinking more and more about marriage.

Commenting on meeting your partner's brother:

What you said: Why didn't you tell me that when you said he lived in Elmira, you meant the Elmira Correctional Facility?

What you could have said: I've never been inside the
slammer before.

Raising the subject of commitment:

What you said: You get six months. Then you're out on
your ass.

What you could have said: It's like going down a road that I
don't want to go down alone. I'm ready to take the next step.

When you make a proper disclosure, you may notice your
partner has more warmth and empathy and is less jumpy and
defensive. The interaction is warmer. Here, it becomes easier to
see just how much disclosure can change the nature of the conversation and the tone of the relationship. To really get closer,
however, you'll want to work your way into higher risk disclosures about being together *when you are together*—otherwise
known as here and now disclosures.

The Risks and the Power of Here and Now Disclosures

As you become more involved with your prospective bride
or groom, you realize that nothing compares to the high-pitched
drama of falling for someone who is falling for you. Goofy and
starry-eyed, you feel like you are awakening from a deep sleep.
You begin, perhaps for the first time in your adult life, to feel
validated for existing, limitless in your capacity to feel love, and
complete in your sense of self. Thus, the world becomes a more
tender place, a place where you'll want to make more disclosures because you are ready to:

- take more risks
- share more of who you really are
- be yourself and know yourself through loving and being
  loved—even when it means being vulnerable

- become closer
- be more stimulated and stimulating
- surprise yourself and be surprised

Here and now disclosures make all these things happen because they are about the live energy that exists between the two of you in the moment. That is what also makes them scary. In a here and now disclosure, you are addressing your partner and the relationship directly. It's done with the idea of offering more of yourself—an offering in the moment that reflects your *thoughts* and/or *feelings* toward him and *why you think you feel that way*. Like this:

> I'm so glad to be with you because I laugh so much. I'm a little nervous because you're cute and cute men make me shy.

> I wish I didn't get scared because I worry that the way I act when I'm scared will scare you away. I don't want that to happen.

> Every time we get together, I feel closer to you because you make everything easy.

 Disclosure:
I worried when we didn't speak.
I get excited when I see you.
I'm nervous.

Not a disclosure:
Why didn't you call me?
Are you glad to see me?
You make me nervous.

The wonderful surprise is that making proper disclosures takes your focus off finding the right person. *You become the right person.* Disclosures we thought would be scary turn out to be exhilarating—closeness is exhilarating. The more we disclose, the more positive response we get to our disclosures, and the more alive and energetic we feel in each other's presence. *But there's one more thing that you must know. This will make it or break it for most couples.*

Timing of Disclosures

Symmetry starts love.
Empathy makes love safer.
Disclosure cements love.
but
In order to cement love, disclosures must be properly timed and balanced.

A well-timed disclosure can make her throw herself into your arms. The ill-timed disclosure can make her throw herself in front of a herd of stampeding cattle. Thus, you must understand the difference between the *desire* to disclose and the *drive* to get something off your chest. For example, several years ago Kevin was driving Ursula to a lecture she was giving. She was pretty nervous, and he was very kind in bolstering her ego. This was a moment when they both knew that the relationship was getting more serious. In fact, they were getting closer and closer to making love, and Kevin still had not told her that he had herpes. He knew he ought to tell her very soon. He knew she needed to know this fact. The closeness he felt to her in that moment made him feel nervous because she might reject him when she found out. Just as they were about to arrive at the place where Ursula was speaking, she thanked him for being so supportive. Then, she winked and invited him back to her place after the lecture. She smiled seductively. Kevin responded by blurting out, *"I have herpes."*

That is an example of the drive to get something off your chest. Of course, he was nervous. It's understandable. And of course, Ursula was flabbergasted by his unfortunate timing. As for you, if you have something important to communicate, you may need the following guide to timing:

Don't disclose: when you are on the way to meet her parents and/or friends, etc. This is not the time to say, "By the way, did I mention that I have three kids from three previous marriages?"

Do disclose: when you are sitting peacefully together and you feel she is in an empathic state.

Don't disclose: when you are in bed having sex. This is not the time to say, "I've never had an orgasm."

Do disclose: when you are sitting peacefully together and you feel she is particularly empathic.

Don't disclose: when you have been drinking heavily. This is not the time to tell her you were incarcerated for petty larceny.

Do disclose: when you are sitting peacefully together and you feel she is particularly empathic.

 When I met my husband I found out early on that he was five years younger than I was and that he had never been married. I, on the other hand, had been through two, yes, two marriages while I was still in my twenties. I was afraid to tell him because it seemed logical that he would reject me. I was pretty sure it wouldn't sit well with him. I made a big fuss in my head about getting the facts out. When I told him, he couldn't have cared less. The subject never came up again unless I brought it up.

Of course you have a few skeletons or eccentricities. We all do. When she's had the chance to know some less loaded things about you, and you sense her genuine interest in knowing you better; when she's had a chance to see how nice her quality of life is when you are in it, this is a time to begin low-risk disclosures and make progress from there.

On the other hand, if you have something really important for her to know right up front because you imagine that it will have a major impact on whether the two of you get together, something such as the fact that you are separated but not divorced or that you have children or whatever *you know matters*, then spare yourself the anxiety. Tell her what you have to tell her when you are sitting peacefully together and you feel she is particularly empathic. Don't let it go past the first few dates or you will ruin your own good time.

Lightning Fast Disclosures

Once I led a workshop in Connecticut in which the group started off by introducing themselves to each other. One woman explained she was recently widowed at thirty-seven. Another woman in this small group had also just lost her husband, so she spoke right up. The two women had lunch together and over lunch, they shared a lifetime. They returned to the seminar as best friends.

Disclosures can be appropriate or inappropriate. For the women above, symmetry, empathy, and disclosure converged quickly into a welcome, intimate bond. Sometimes we click in an instant and remain together for life.

More often, disclosures come slowly, and, in order to cement a bond, disclosures must be shared and balanced. The biggest mistake you can make is when he says, "So, tell me about yourself," and you tell and tell and tell believing that because he encouraged you, he must want to know. At the end of the evening, you're so overexposed that you may as well be running naked at the Grammys, while he is so underexposed that he will decide you're too complicated, too full of yourself, too messed up. The fact that he asked you will never occur to him. Yes, it's true. As with many good intentions, you gave him more than he wanted, more than he could handle.

> Never be so messed up that you don't leave room to find
> out how messed up he is.

The Formula for Balanced Disclosures

Say, for example, that you want to know where you stand with
him. You can't just come out and ask him. The proper way to always know where you stand is by making a disclosure, letting
him know in a small way, at first, where you stand. Like this:

1. You offer a here and now disclosure one or two times.

You're fun to be with. I can't remember when I laughed so
much at someone's jokes.

2. You wait until he makes a matching offer.

Does he say, "I'm having fun, too"? Does he squeeze your
hand? Does he sit there silently? Do his eyes dart around the
room? Does he slump over in his chair? Does he excuse himself
to call his mother?

3. If he makes a matching disclosure, you are on the same wavelength.

Wait until the end of the evening or even the next date and
repeat the procedure.

4. If your disclosure is not returned, wait.

You may try once again later, but, if your disclosure is not
matched, there are two possibilities. One is that he's shy. That
means he's not ready to respond yet. Giving him more time is a
good idea. The other possibility is that he does not feel the same
thing you feel. Continuing to disclose to a person who is not as
enthusiastic as you are can only make that person uncomfort-

able in your presence. If you keep doing it, discomfort can turn, ever so quickly, into hate. That, he may disclose.

 If you want an honest relationship, then you must make it safe for him to be honest.

Disclosure Misfires

Every day mistakes are made in the name of disclosure. Here are the three most common culprits.

1. Being honest. (My honesty may kill you, but . . .)

. During lovemaking Carol noticed that Lyle did not seem as deeply involved with her pleasure as he usually was. She stopped the action and said, "Mr. Johnson leaves me cold tonight." Lyle, a bit shocked, said, "What?" Carol replied, "You're not hot so I'm not hot. It's not happening for me."

For Carol, what's on her lung is on her tongue. While she would say that her honesty comes from calling things as they are, in truth, her honesty comes from impulsivity. She doesn't take time to confirm her hunch or to ask a few questions. She senses something, she gets anxious, and she blurts out what comes first to her mind and calls it honesty.

Carol confuses honesty with brutality. She thinks she must openly express all her feelings, and this turns honesty into a way to humiliate and/or gain power over others. Truth ceases to be a gift in her hands. Honesty, without compassion, is a weapon.

2. Disclosures about sex: Does he really want the answers?

Shaniqua felt so comfortable with Miles that, when he asked her about her previous partners, she started to tell him. Then, thinking better of it, she said, "C'mon Miles. You don't want to know this." "I do," Miles replied. "Nothing could change how I feel for you."

Nothing can change how Miles feels about Shaniqua, but something could change the motion pictures he runs in his head about her. They can change from "Shaniqua, the Love Goddess, Meets Miles, the Hung One" to "Shaniqua, the Love Slut, Meets the Third Division and the L.A. Rams." Believe me, your partner can tell you he doesn't care, but his unconscious may care. He may not be able to control how his unconscious manages the information you give him. You just can't know where that information will lead him, especially if some of these guys are still your friends.

 Preoccupation with intimacy is like the preoccupations with simultaneous orgasm. All it will get you is frustration and disappointment.

You don't need to lie. You only need to think more carefully about this kind of information. We often beg to know more, and then become fixated on stories that can only make our relationship more difficult.

3. Anxious flooding: relationship spendthrifts.

Grace chatters on about the menu, the music, the service. During dessert she talks nonstop about mousse, muffins, meringue. Paul finally reaches for her napkin, shreds it, and stuffs his ears with napkin wads. Grace does not take the hint. Instead, she launches into a history of ear canal disasters.

Grace cannot quite get in touch with the warmth that Paul feels for her, and this makes her anxious. Talking is her way of trying to vent her anxiety. She is what is called a flooder, a nonstop talker. Her belief is that, as long as she is speaking, Paul can't slip away.

The big problem, besides driving Paul crazy, is that there isn't much of the real Grace in this conversation. The talk is a smoke screen Grace hides behind. Paul is so overwhelmed by the flooding behavior that he has no idea of who Grace really is.

Talking can just as easily tell *less* about you when it is unrelated, unbalanced, inappropriate. Grace needs to learn how to have a conversation about her anxiety instead of using it as a weapon to keep people away. If she could talk about it, she might make room for warmth to grow. If you know this is your problem, then a careful exploration of your anxiety, along with developing other methods to bind it, is the work that lies ahead.

Or, you could find a partner that likes it. Some people like a chatterer.

Last Thoughts

If you cringed during this chapter, join the many of us who have thrown a pie in the face of love. Then, stop making improper disclosures, even if you have to excuse yourself to the rest room fourteen times to get control.

 Debra was Rush Limbaugh's makeup artist. Stuart was Rush Limbaugh's bodyguard. They noticed each other every night, from opposite sides of the room, but they were both too shy to speak. Months passed before they spoke. They became friends. Then they became lovers. Today, they are married and have a blended family. Neither one works for Rush anymore. I call that a happy ending.

Disclosure Evaluation

As you think about disclosures, ask yourself the following questions:

Are my disclosures the kind that illuminates a situation?

What do I feel right before I disclose?

Does my honesty enhance an intimate connection or improve my relationships?

How do people generally respond to me when I talk?

Have there been times when I've expressed my feelings honestly and things went really well? What was happening then? How did I do that?

> REMEMBER: Unless your disclosures are matched, keep your mouth shut about your deeper self for the rest of the date.

Good marriages are marriages where the couple creates a safe environment for balanced disclosures.

If you want to feel safe then you must make the relationship a safe place to be.

Love Blunders

You Owe Me

When Jillian met Joe, he was in rough emotional shape. He came from an abusive background, and he was a substance abuser. Jillian got him to attend Narcotics Anonymous, and she stuck by him. Eventually Joe felt more secure about his recovery, and he went back to college and got a diploma. Soon after, he got a great job that required much of his energy. Jillian attended his office Christmas party, where quite a few people came over to tell her how much they loved working with Joe. Jillian began to recount the story of what Joe was like when she met him. Joe began nudging her. When they got in the car to go home, he told her how hurt he felt and how angry. She snapped that if it hadn't been for her, he'd still be smoking pot on a mattress thrown on the living room floor.

The blunder: You owe what you are to me and my love.

The good intention: A safe relationship offers self-repair. I offered you that.

The flaw: If I don't get credit, I feel upset. If you don't think you're nothing without me, then you could dump me at any moment. I'll keep you thinking I'm responsible for what is good in your life as a way of getting you to marry me.

The step toward the aisle: I want to find it a pleasure to watch you blossom. In my weaker moments when I feel threatened by your progress, I'll talk with you about it, rather than trying to subvert you. Also, I will pay more attention to the things I owe you since there are many that I'm underappreciating.

4

The Fourth Step
Down the Aisle

Exclusivity

Carla and Jimmy have dated for five months. They spend every weekend together. They talk on the phone twice a day. They are happy. It goes without saying that she has a committed relationship . . . doesn't it?

Vivian waited in line for hours to buy two very expensive concert tickets for her favorite band. She decided to surprise Jeff with them, but the surprise was on her when Jeff said he *hated* that music. Vivian woke up the next morning wondering—if she could be so wrong about a band, what other assumptions had she made about Jeff?

Denise knows that Tom is the one. Does Tom know?

In a budding relationship, it becomes apparent after a point that the two of you are a couple. Your friends and family know, your office mates know, your exes know, everyone knows. It naturally develops, and in many cases nothing more can be said about it. However, at some point, you'll want to hear the words out loud because:

You've been waiting to hear them all your life.

You aren't sure where things stand even though he's not seeing anyone else.

Your friends hound you that he didn't say it.

A little voice in your head wakes you up at night.

You think he still sees himself as available.

You've been dating him for a l-o-n-g time and if he can't say it soon, you're going to dump him and move on.

It makes sense, after a few months, to seek clarity. How you go about getting that clarity constitutes the fourth step down the aisle.

Three Facts About Men and Commitment

Although men are equally desirous for marriage and a long life together, they have more trouble than women with making articulated, formal commitments. And they have good reasons.

1. Synonyms for "commitment" are "duty," "obligation," "guarantee," and "mortgage."

Men never hear the word "commitment" without hearing its synonyms. Although "duty" is just a four-letter word, it can seem overwhelming to him. When women hear "commitment" we have fuzzy feelings about a cozy love. When men hear "commitment" they hear mortgage, second job, health insurance, complicated taxes, burden, a nubile daughter who is starting to date boys, no more late poker nights with the guys. How can you can let him know that commitment doesn't have to be a burden—that you are as competent as he is?

2. "Commitment" equals "loss."

Dwight adored Samantha, and, in practice, he loved being with her. However, in theory, becoming exclusive with Samantha meant he would no longer be able to toy with Francine, Joelle, Margarita, and Winnie. The fact that he would never be with any of them anyway doesn't matter. Dwight would no longer have the choice. That is what matters. Giving up other women is not the problem—giving up *the choice* is the problem. Choosing Samantha means *not being free to choose anyone else* whether he wants them or not.

 New Meaning to "Bearing" Witness
Janet, a state park ranger, met Randy, a forest ranger. They fell in love and decided to marry. After considering the usual options for last names, they nixed them all. Instead, they decided to change *both* their last names to "Park" because that was where they met.

---

3. Chasing is more intense than winning.

When we fall in love, much of our passion quivers around the fact that our partner is unknown to us. Her sexual turn-ons are a deep mystery, and mystery intensifies passion and increases the possibility of having your socks knocked off. Does she believe in the G spot? Does she have a G spot? Could I find her G spot? What does she wear to bed? When he wins you, certain mysteries begin to subside, and a bit of the passion fades with it. Men tend to place a higher value on winning than women do, and men tend to use winning as a source of validation. Thus, winning means the end of chasing. Some men need time to adjust.

Three facts about women and commitment:

1. We want one.
2. Sooner is better than later.
3. Later will do.

What to Do If You Want to Wear White Before Next Winter

If you've been waiting to hear words you haven't heard yet, then you're in trouble—not because you haven't heard the words, but because your strategy is chronically passive. The decision to make your relationship exclusive is not a passive one. Women often put themselves in the "waiting" position, hoping he'll get the hint. What you need is a plan.

1. Remember why he fell for you in the first place.

When he met you, he knew that his life was going to be richer and more interesting if you were in it. Why? I'll say it again—why? He wanted you because you had a life before he met you. He wanted you because you were sexy, smart, playful, engaged by life. Have you sacrificed these traits in yourself, *the very things that drew him to you out of all others,* in the interest of the relationship and found that it's backfired?

 The Puritans described marriage as "the little church within the Church." Thus, every day was a chance to love and a chance to forgive.

---

2. Figure out why you ended the chase before the finish line.

Does he come over every Friday and stay till Sunday? Do you always check with him before making other plans with friends? Are you always available, always ready, always making his life easier and thinking you should be rewarded for it? If so, think again. Passive, passive, passive. You've made it easy for him not to do anything. *Don't play manipulative games, but don't win the "Doormat of the Year" award either.*

 If he has no anxiety, he has no reason to do anything different than he's doing now. If everything is perfect, why should he tamper with it?

---

3. Bring the life back into your love.

You can, without playing any stupid games, re-create the feeling of the chase, simply by changing your routine. Visit your old friend from college. Get those season tickets for you and your sister. Pick a great project to throw your heart and soul into. Make plans with him, and make plans with others. Remind him how much you love him, and then go meet your friends for dinner. By bringing the life back into yourself you bring the life back into your love, thereby reminding him of why he had to have you, why he must take steps to ensure he'll always have you.

4. Pose a question to yourself about yourself out loud.

This technique is my personal favorite. Hundreds of hubbies have been caught with it—if he doesn't drag you off to a shrink. Since this is hard to describe, here's an example.

You are sitting together in a quiet moment. Things are sweet between you. Speak to yourself out loud and say:
I dunno, Susie (only if your name is Susie), he's cute, he's sweet, you're smitten. What are you going to do? Run? Stay? Call in the second team?
or

When he leaves, you miss him. What if you've already fallen for him? Should you tell Brad, Leo, and the Hanson brothers that you can't take their calls?

It can never be a question or comment to him. It must be a question to yourself about yourself. This kind of comment can lead the discussion into the area of an exclusive commitment.

> NOTE: If you try it a few times and it doesn't work, *stop immediately* or he may start calling you Sybil.

4. Pull his leg.

Tell him you realize that he's been hinting at making it exclusive for months now. Say you were hesitant at first, unsure. But now you realize he was right all along, and so you want to help him out. Tell him you're sorry you made him wait so long, but you had to be sure you were ready. Then, sigh and say, "I know, I know. You love me. It's all right, you don't have to worry anymore."

We Have an Understanding

However you get there, the two of you should have an understanding. At some point, your understanding needs to be verbalized so that both of you know for sure that you are on the same wavelength. If you aren't sure what "an understanding" means, here are the guidelines to follow so you both understand your understanding.

We understand that:
1. We don't sleep with others.
2. We will inform each other reasonably about plans that will affect the other—things such as vacations, holidays, late nights out.

3. This relationship could lead to marriage, and, if things continue, this is our plan.

4. Since marriage is in our thoughts, we agree to make time to talk about our hopes for our future and our ideas about how we see our lives unfolding. This includes conversations about religion, child rearing, retirement, money, in-laws, and all of the kinds of things couples need to consider when they are marriage-bound.

5. If we survive these conversations, then it's time to send out invitations.

Name   Date

_____   _____

_____   _____

Emergency Plan to Handle a Noncommittal Partner

1. Never whine, never whimper. You're better than that.

 Darla wooed Jimmy. He told her he liked her, but he wasn't ready to settle down. When he got transferred from North Dakota to Atlanta, she moved, too. Everyone thought she was nuts. And then, one day, Jimmy saw the light and they got married. She saw through his ambivalence, and she hung in there. Things like this do happen.

---

2. Carefully consider your timing and choose a moment to talk when he is open to conversation.

3. Using your own words, say, "The more time we spend together, the more my feelings grow. For me, this is the

kind of road I don't want to go down alone. So, it would help me to know where you are."

4. Be silent. Wait. Don't dilute your message by continuing to talk.

5. If he can't speak to it, tell him it's okay for him to think about it and get back to you. Ask him how long he needs.

6. If he still can't answer, pick a date in your head for how long you can wait for him to decide. Tell him you want to speak about it again in one, two, three months.

7. *Don't bring up the topic until that date.*

8. Figure out the best use of your time until that date.

9. If, on that date, he still has no answer, you must decide how long you want to put up with his ambivalence. Is it worth the risk? Is he just on a different timetable?

10. Ask him what he thinks you should do.

11. Continue your life.

12. You may, if you wish, repeat all the steps. If he is still unable to move in any direction and this is unsatisfactory, let him know you need to make a decision about this for yourself. Again, ask him if he has any input. Listen carefully to his response.

13. Consider three sessions of couples therapy for the purposes of clarifying the relationship for both of you.

14. Maintain your dignity.

15. Follow through on your part of the bargain no matter how difficult. If you don't, the message to him is that there are no consequences to his actions. He can do whatever he wants, and you'll still be there.

16. If you've tried everything and nothing has worked, it is time to feel free to rant and rave. You have no dignity left so what have you got to lose? Leave long messages on his machine using up all his free space. Call all his friends. Call Jerry Springer. Emote.

17. Dump the turd. Weep. Start dating again.

PART II

Why Aren't You Married Yet?

CHAPTER 5

You're Already Spoken For

Priscilla's warm and loving parents are so warm and loving that she didn't move out until she was twenty-nine. Four years later her dad still drops off toilet paper and paper towels at her apartment.

Jerry dated several women, none longer than six months. With his many good qualities, he can't fathom why nothing clicks. He came to therapy for guidance, and, when his history was being taken, he mentioned that both of his parents were Holocaust survivors, but he's sure this has nothing to do with his problem.

Larry and his mom speak on the phone every day at ten A.M. and again at seven P.M. Mostly, Larry's mother complains about Larry's father. Last week when Larry was in a meeting, his mother called three times until Larry came back to his office.

Are you *supposed* to get married? Or could you be one of the thousands of eligible, appealing adults who date, make love, place personal ads, and get your heart broken *without ever realizing that you have an unconscious mandate not to marry?* If you believe that you want to get married, yet nothing seems to click, consider the possibility that someone has a previous claim on you, and you don't even know it. In fact, that person may not know it either.

A previous claim on you means that you've gotten a silent message not to marry. The claim can be laid by someone who really wants you to be happy and who, if this theory were put before them, would not know what you are talking about. It can also be laid by self-centered people in your life who consider you a satellite to them and put their needs before yours . . . always. Either way, it doesn't affect the outcome. You may want to marry. You may meet people who want to marry you. But, somehow, it doesn't work out. This quiz will help clarify.

Are You Supposed to Marry?

Rate each statement 1–5.

1 = never

2 = rarely

3 = sometimes

4 = often

5 = it's chronic

Your mom/dad says:

_____ "That's your date? Oh, c'mon, you can do better than that."

_____ "You'll never find anyone as wonderful as your mom/dad, let alone anyone who will love/understand you like your mom/dad does."

_____ "Where were you? I've been calling you all day. I left two messages on your answering machine."

Your mom/dad:

_____   maintains a limited social life with few friends.

_____   designates you as his/her best sounding board for help
with major and minor decisions.

_____   suffers depression due to a major loss or traumatic event
(at any point in life).

You:

_____   don't see the point of protesting when your mom
comes over and organizes your apartment, hems your
new jeans, does a load of laundry, and cooks your meals
for the week, carefully freezing them in separate
packages.

_____   feel guilty if you don't call to say hello or update your
mom/dad frequently because they so enjoy hearing
about your life and giving you advice about it.

_____   are bothered by the fact that you're over twenty-four and
still living with your parents.

You:

_____   feel upset and/or guilty if you get angry with your
mom/dad, after all, how can you be mad at someone
who does so much for you and tries so hard?

_____   invite a woman you really like back to your place.
In the middle of a great kiss your mother's voice
sounds from your answering machine. "Norman, are
you there? Norman, pick up the phone. I know you're
there."

_____   watch your previous dates move on to marry other people,
sometimes very quickly after breaking up with you.

Add up your score.

12–16:　You probably aren't speaking to your parents anyway.

17–23:　You don't have this problem, but you may date someone who does. So read on anyway.

24–30:　Your mom/dad was most comfortable when they were the center of your universe and want to keep it that way.

31–35:　You're still calling your parents "ma ma" and "da da."

36–60:　You and your mom still wear those mother/daughter matching outfits even though you are over thirty-five.

Why This Happens

With whom did you have your first major, impassioned love affair? If you answered "Ricardo, the waiter at Club Med," think again. The correct answer is your parents. When you are born your parents exist to gratify your needs, anticipate your moods, give you food, warmth, praise, comfort, love.

We see our parents as existing to help us, supply us, focus on us. For a scraped knee, a new pair of sneakers, emotional support, a ride to softball practice—we count on our parents to provide. Vestiges of this first love affair stay with us. Perhaps you call Mom when your boyfriend looks at you cross-eyed, maybe you expect your parents to give you a down payment for your first home, or to pay your tuition when you decide to go back to school in your thirties. A part of us imagines our parents exist to help us as they did when we were little. It can be very hard to cut the cord.

When we fall in love we transfer many of these feelings from our parents to our partner. In this way, we truly separate from our parents and master a major developmental task of our lives; therefore, even if the love affair doesn't work out, our relationship with our parents will never be quite the same again. That's part of why Moms wears waterproof mascara when you walk down the aisle. Sure, she's delighted that you won't be coming to dinner with your laundry anymore, but she's also aware that she is no longer number one—she feels loss. At your wedding, you symbolically leave your parents behind and make someone else first in your life.

 Oh, Nurse . . .
The late Senator Barry Goldwater, despondent over the death of his wife, did not want to remarry. He became ill and when his doctor was unable to make a house call, the doctor sent a nurse named Susan to take the Senator's blood pressure. They talked. They laughed. They fell in love. They married.

When Something Goes Wrong with This Sequence

That's how it's *supposed* to work. But, sometimes, your parents aren't ready to give you up, or even share you with someone else. Moreover, something in your own life can happen so that, psychologically and/or physically, you don't want to leave your parents.

Most of the time this is not about cruelty or manipulation by your parents, although that can be the case. It is about our difficulty separating from someone we've deeply loved and their difficulty separating from us. The examples in the beginning of this chapter are of families who have not managed to separate successfully. Let's rejoin them to understand three reasons why this happens:

1. You are put on a pedestal by a parent.

Priscilla has always gotten everything she ever wanted, when she wanted it, from her parents: the clothes she wanted when she wanted them, an ever-listening ear from her mother, a feeling of unconditional love from her dad. She's such a good kid, though, and such a good daughter, that no one would ever think to call her spoiled. Her parents are her best friends—she always knows that she can count on them. It's wonderful in many, many ways to feel this loved; it's splendid; and it's a big part of why pretty Prissy can't hook up with a guy. No man can ever match her parents' love. No man can ever give her that much.

2. Your family has had a tragic loss.

Jerry's parents met after World War II. They were both in concentration camps where his father lost his entire family and his mother lost her first husband and her parents. Understandably, Jerry feels too guilty to express his own needs and losses. How do you tell parents who were in a concentration camp that you feel blue? How guilty do you feel if you get angry at your parents after what they've been through? Jerry's spent a lifetime holding in his feelings.

Jerry gets two messages from his parents. They speak of carrying on the family as the most important thing in the world. And, although his parents want him to marry, he unconsciously feels that they would experience his marriage as one more loss. Besides, they are old now. If he takes a wife, she would have to come first, and how can he say no to his folks?

3. You are your parent's closest confidante.

Larry and his mother are buds. In fact, it's been that way since Larry was little. His mom confided in him about everything—even sex. When his mom and dad had a fight, he would take his mom into his bedroom to comfort her. The thing is, Larry is thirty-two now, and his mom still wants to come first.

She calls, she drops over unexpectedly, she has the key to Larry's apartment. And although Larry gets irritated at his mom, he can't seem to get the intrusions under control. If Larry were to marry, he would have to put a wife first, and, on some unconscious level, he's not sure how his mom would take that.

Priscilla, Jerry, and Larry want to marry, but years go by and they don't.

 In the 1500s marriages took place without witnesses or ceremonies. The Council of Trent decreed in 1563 that marriages were celebrations requiring the presence of a priest and at least two witnesses. They wanted to prevent sinful procreation, although they did not see any necessity for love.

What to Do If You Don't Think You Can Change Things, but You Still Want to Get Married

Why not find a partner who is also smothered by her parents? A woman who still lives at home? A man who's not ashamed to go to his twenty-year high school reunion with his mother on his arm? A gal whose mother has not learned English even though they've been in this country for over twenty-five years so she has to write all her mom's checks and make her doctor appointments?

Don't laugh. A lot of you are in the same boat, if you would only set out to find each other. Someone knows exactly what you go through. It may even be possible to have one big happy family.

NOTE: Do not consider walking down the aisle until all six of you have agreed in advance where you will spend the next sixteen Thanksgivings and Christmas Eves!

Six Degrees of Separation from Your Parents

If you decide to find a partner and make him the number one man in your life, the following steps map out what you will have to do:

1. Face the bottom line.

Your parent, for whatever the reason, does not want to let you go. You, for whatever reason, have agreed to go along with this. You love your parents. That's a given. Also a given is that your parents probably don't have much incentive to change your relationship with them. You do, so don't expect their help— at least for a while.

 Written in the Stars
One week before his scheduled vacation with Carla, Derek was offered the most important gig of his life. Carla, disappointed but understanding, decided to go with a girlfriend of hers. During the vacation, Derek called to speak with the girlfriend. He told her that she had to have Carla on the beach the next day at noon because he had a surprise planned. The next day as they were lying on the beach, a plane appeared above them and began skywriting:
CARLA, WILL YOU MARRY ME? DEREK

---

2. Begin the process of separation.

Demote your parents. Try the following:

• Make fewer and shorter phone calls and/or visits home.
• Accept fewer and shorter phone calls and/or visits.

- Take your stuff out of storage at your parents' house.
- Do your own laundry (taxes, checkbook, cleaning).
- Stop spending your weekends there—even if they do have a pool.
- Call a friend when you need advice or support.
- Don't be a go-between for your parents' relationship.
- Stop telling your parents *everything*.

3. Feel awful.

In addition to temporarily feeling awful, you can add in lonely, guilty, angry, and depressed. Those feelings are just about right—you are where you should be. Don't worry. It's gonna pass.

> NOTE: Learning to tolerate feeling awful and having awful feelings is an important lesson for marriage. There will be times in a marriage when you will not like your partner very much, when she will not like you very much, and when the potential to get into an ugly fight is very seductive. If you can wait it through without retaliating if you feel attacked, it will be very helpful later on.

4. Keep up your courage.

Don't expect your mom/dad to welcome these changes with open arms. If they do, terrific. But, if you make changes in the relationship, you can expect that your parent will experience the loss and the loneliness, too. Mom's headaches get worse, Dad sulks, your mother and father argue more . . . don't get sucked in and don't go back to your old ways.

You will have to figure out how to handle them. This is vital to your availability for marriage as well as to your marriage once you have it.

So, tell your mom you love her, but you can't come for dinner every Sunday because, on some Sundays, your girlfriend will have slept over and you want to be alone with her. And, on some other Sundays, you need to be alone. And then, stick to your guns unless there is a life-threatening emergency.

5. Continue to love your parent, even if you can't like her right now.

If your parent gets angry with you, say, "I can see you are upset, and I know anything I say now will only make it worse. I love you, but this is how it has to be."

6. Find a marriage partner.

You are now ready to date and work toward marriage. Don't bring her home too soon to meet your folks. Don't avoid spending a weekend with your girlfriend because you were supposed to have dinner at your mom's. Turn on your answering machine when your boyfriend is over. Don't tell your folks all about your girlfriend until the relationship is stable, and, *above all*, don't ever, ever take a taste of your girlfriend's special pasta dish and say, "My mother always uses cheese."

 Build a nurturing team.
One way to get through a rough time is to nurture a few friendships with people who know what you want for your life and who want to help you get it. And vice versa.

Debunking a Love Myth

Myth: The greatest lovers are Romeo and Juliet, Abelard and Heloise, Cathy and Heathcliff.

The half truth: They loved each other a lot.

The danger: You get swept away by doomed love and start thinking that romance walks hand in hand with suffering. You get hooked on turbulence.

The reality: Happy love has no history, and happy lovers do not capture our interest. However, having lots of intense feelings does not ensure that your relationship will last. It does not even ensure that your relationship is about love. Yes, couples can endure the worst traumas, but trauma tears more couples apart than it binds for life.

What you can learn from this: Don't get sucked in by anguished couples, feeble from love, and forced to give up life, limb, and occasional genitalia for the experience. Make that story your television movie of the week, not your life.

CHAPTER 6

You Scare Them Away

He goes on a three-week business trip and doesn't call you often enough. She wakes up cranky and nothing you do seems to cheer her up. He wants a winter wedding and voices it with clarity and conviction, and you still can't believe that he *really* loves you. Do angry feelings frighten you? Is temporary separation perceived as abandonment? Do your partner's occasional bad moods make you feel that she's about to dump you? It is natural to feel at times as if you aren't getting enough attention. Sometimes it's hard to believe that we'll ever get enough. We all can be a little love-hungry, and our insecurities take many shapes, such as:

lecturing

overdoing good deeds

endless discussions about "the relationship"

constant testing of your partner's love

clinging

We adopt these behaviors when all we really want is reassurance that we are loved. Our need for reassurance can be as strong as our need to eat. We feel "hungry." Not the hunger you feel when you get the irrepressible urge for a Snickers, but a driven hunger, where people grab whatever is at hand because who knows when they'll eat again. The key difference with this kind of hunger is that, even as they swallow, they can't enjoy food because they are preparing for future deprivation—the time when they will be hungry again.

You can have emotional hunger in which you are as hungry for attention as another person can be for food. Emotional hunger is the root of many insecure feelings in a relationship. The following quiz will tell you more.

Circle one.

When I get upset

1   I want my partner with me.

2   I feel lost if my partner isn't around.

3   I feel desperate to be close to my partner.

As our relationship continues

1   though occasionally anxious, I enjoy getting closer.

2   I worry frequently that I will be rejected.

3   I can't enjoy getting closer because I'm scared.

When my partner takes off on his own

1   I miss him.

2   I get angry that he left me out.

3   I feel abandoned.

I put my partner's needs

1   beside my own.

2   before my own.

3   I can't get on with my own stuff if my partner has a problem.

I do things for my partner

(1)   as part of being a couple.

2   because it makes me feel important.

3   because I fear he will reject me if I don't.

When I wonder if our love will last

1   I feel confident that it will.

(2)   I get scared that it will not.

3   I live in fear that we will break up.

When it comes to my feelings

1   my partner understands me.

2   my partner seems to understand me most of the time.

(3)   I rarely feel heard or understood.

When I need reassurance I

1   feel confident that my partner can comfort me.

(2)   sometimes feel frustrated instead of comforted by my partner.

3   can't be consoled.

Add up your score.

8–10:   Push back from the banquet table, emotional hunger isn't a problem for you.

11–17:   Read on, and remember: Most of us fall into this category.

18–24:   You could be smothering your relationship with your needs. Don't be alarmed. This chapter will offer you resources to help you trust yourself more.

Women, Men, and Emotional Hunger

Many people mistakenly assume that emotional hunger is only a woman's issue. They think that women pursue closeness from men who are ambivalent, so that our need for closeness is never satisfied. The stereotype says she wants to hold on to the relationship more than he does—that, for women, any relationship is better than no relationship. Like any stereotype, this is demeaning.

 Combined Dating Service/Wedding
How about the man who was so sick of being asked when he was going to get married that he set a wedding date without having a bride? He placed an ad stating his wedding date, and a large number of prospective brides responded. His friends picked a woman for him—a woman he'd never met. The two of them were married a day later in the Mall of America.

NOTE: Emotional hunger should not be confused with the fact that women tend to feel closest when our mate is in the room or in our arms. We like lots of closeness and we have a wonderfully uncanny longing to know more about the emotional lives of others. That's our nature, and aren't we lucky!

In truth, both men and women experience emotional hunger in profound ways. Women just feel freer to talk about it more. Here are the words of men:

I think of Diana as providence, and I can't get going without her. I lost my mother when I was fifteen. When I met Diana, I felt relaxed for the first time since my mother died.

I turned to Diana for everything. When she decided to go to night school and she was away from home so much, I thought I was going crazy.

Mindy is my life. On the weekends, she sleeps late, sometimes all day. I sit in the living room in the dark, and I wait for her to wake up. I just sit there, feeling so lost, listening for the sound of rustling sheets. I can't seem to function. I go into a trance, a deep depression. If she sleeps all day, I sit all day. I don't eat—nothing would taste good.

The Roots of Emotional Hunger for Men and Women

Hunger is the first longing. All a baby longs for is a mommy with a nipple. A hungry baby is an anxious baby. Hungry babies wail, and when the nipple appears, their anxiety is reduced—they immediately stop crying. But a nipple can't always be produced at the baby's demand. Sometimes we are in the checkout aisle at Kmart. When that happens, the baby is devastated and wails, as if to say, "There is no mother, no food. . . . I am all alone, and I am dying." A baby can't tolerate waiting—a baby can't even process the experience of waiting. To a baby, mother is life.

 Liberace used to receive twelve proposals a week from his fans.

A baby who must wait ten times too many or ten minutes too long (and how can we ever know for each temperament what that is?) will get the feeling that Mother is unresponsive. Depending on other early life experiences, this belief can become: *If Mother is unresponsive, then all people are unresponsive.* No one will be available when I need them. You cannot hold on to love or trust it. There is no security. The child grows up anticipating unresponsiveness from others. So, even when people are both responsive and unresponsive, out of all the interactions with others, they only remember when they were let down. This point of view gets carried into adulthood and acts as the "pocket protector" of relationships. History clicks in. Everyone lets you down.

How to Stop Smothering Love and Start Getting It

Emotional hunger signals that we want more love. The following examples explain how this takes shape in our relationships and what to do about it.

1. Overdoing good deeds.

Danielle runs Tom's errands, cooks gourmet meals, massages his feet, wears makeup to bed, remembers to send a birthday card to his mother. Tom used to think it was great, but, lately, he's been edgy. In her attempt to make it impossible to live without her, Danielle is driving Tom nuts.

Five Signs That You Are Overdoing It
- Your partner snaps at you when you are "only trying to help."
- You feel that you are giving a lot more than you are getting.
- You already recognize that you try too hard to please.
- You feel guilty taking pleasure for yourself (e.g., you rarely have the first orgasm).
- You do a lot for your partner and hope he'll reciprocate.

Whenever Ursula, a client in one of my therapy groups, desperately needs the group's attention for an important matter in her life, she instead comes into the group and offers an inordinate amount of attention to others. She begins by praising others, and once, when someone needed to borrow cab fare from her, she refused to be paid back. Since the group has begun to recognize her pattern they refuse to let her continue it. Ursula is learning that she has pent-up anger toward others from the imbalance she creates because, deep down, her giving so much comes from a hope that others could give back to her when she needs it. Yet, until she learns to ask for help, others rarely pick up on her cues and she feels disappointed in people.

What to Do If This Is You

If you run yourself ragged for love, ask yourself:

- What do you think would happen if you stopped?
- If you weren't spending so much time doing things for your partner, what would you be doing instead?
- How do you think your partner would respond if you put more time into yourself?
- Do you have a history of playing the same role in other relationships, including family relationships, or did you grow up with a model of another family member doing this?
- When *you* need comfort, how do you ask for it?

If you find this all too familiar:

Replace one thing you do for him with something you do for yourself. The following week, replace two, etc.

See what it feels like. Notice how your partner and others respond. Keep at this until the balance is more reasonable. Don't be surprised when he starts to like you better.

What If Your Partner Does Too Much for You

- Tell her directly that she's overdoing it, and you want her to cut back because it is making you uncomfortable.
- Recognize that your partner has a strong need for approval. Her good deeds are like a hundred "Hail Mary"s. Maybe she was taught that anger is bad, and no one loves a bad girl. Even when she doesn't really feel like being good, she cannot permit herself to be bad. She worries because inside, where no one can see, she feels like a hostile, bad person, and she's terrified of being found out. Let her know it's

okay for her to have bad feelings. When she does express them, listen carefully.

 A *Swing* magazine survey notes that forty-six percent of the readers think that a couple should date for one to three years before getting married. Fourteen percent think six months of dating is enough. Two percent say that under six months is enough time to meet and marry the right one.

- Tell her she is irreplaceable, and that you already know that no one would ever be as interested in your welfare as she is, so she doesn't have to work that hard.
- It can be a nice feeling to be so taken care of, but it isn't so good for your partner. Offer to wash her hair, give her a pedicure, run an errand for her.

I had a client, Chantal, whose mother was a prototype for this problem. Her mother refused to accept any gift from Chantal (who is in her forties). She would not let Chantal treat her to dinner, hold the umbrella in the rain, or pay for the toll call. Chantal came into therapy feeling guilty because all her mother wanted was to give, give, give. She couldn't understand her fury toward her mother until she figured out that, in her mother's hands, giving was a way to control as well as a way to hide from having a real relationship with her daughter. In addition, giving and not taking was a way for Chantal's mother to keep Chantal as a little girl: Little girls take from their mommies, little girls need their mommies. If Chantal didn't take and need in the same way she always had, it would mean that her mother would have to redefine the relationship and herself.

2. The boot camp sergeant.

Lena and Matt are preparing a romantic dinner at home. She rearranges the glasses he has set. After he's added salt to the sauce, she adds more. Then, she asks him to chop the tomato for the salad. He chooses a knife and begins slicing. Lena takes the knife out of his hands and starts to show him a better way to slice and dice. "When you do it that way," she explains, "the tomato falls apart." "It's hard to get good help these days," Matt says, and leaves the room.

Five Signs That You'll Never Be Satisfied

- You tell people the right way to do things that they have been doing for themselves for years without the benefit of your input (starting the car, fluffing a pillow).
- People have commented that you are giving unasked-for advice.
- You don't feel as warm and loving as you want to when your partner doesn't do things your way.
- You don't feel satisfied in the relationship.
- You persist in explaining something that is actually absurd, such as the right way to put the toilet paper on the roll.

 Fly Me to the Moon
Larry tied an engagement ring to a kite string and took Samantha kite flying on the beach. As she tugged on the string, the ring came tumbling down. Luckily they found it. She said yes, but wasn't sure she approved of his method.

We all have a little of this. Ann Landers has had entire columns on the proper direction for the toilet paper to be pulled from the toilet paper holder. A single detail takes over the minds of millions. But for Lena, details take the place of the warmth. She does not think about whether Matt makes her heart sing or whether they are happy together or how much she needs him. Instead she thinks about whether or not the towels are being folded correctly, whether the napkins match the tablecloth. She cannot shift her attention away from the fantasy that Martha Stewart is watching over the house, about to drag Lena away to remedial housekeeping hell.

What to Do If This Is You

If you wrote to Ann Landers about the toilet paper, ask yourself:

- What would be happening if I weren't so busy giving orders?
- What would happen if the tomato is improperly sliced and the toilet paper is backward?
- What am I feeling right before I give these orders? Right after?
- How do my partner and other people respond to me?
- Does this bring us closer?

After you've answered these questions, try an alternate-days exercise. Practice one day on and one day off. Give your usual advice on one day and notice how your partner responds to you. On the alternating day, *don't give any advice*. In fact, try giving encouragement at the times you'd have given advice. See if you notice any difference in how he responds to you.

What to Do If This Is Your Partner

- Your partner sees the world as having harsh rules and standards that must constantly be met. She feels pressure. Let her know that Martha Stewart doesn't live in the neighborhood.
- Never ridicule her.
- Ask for her advice—in fact, try asking for lots of advice. She may just get sick of giving it and curb her behavior without your even having to mention it.
- Directly tell her that her constant opinions are making you

defensive. Gently remind her when it happens and ask her to stop.

- Try to find a metaphor or buzzword that lets her know she's doing it again—something that points it out without being cruel. Nancy salutes her husband, Pete, when he starts sounding like a sergeant. Ellen smiles and bows to her husband, Pasquale, when he starts dictating orders like a king.

- Experiment with different ways to let her orders roll off your back since you know they are a function of her own anxiety rather than really being about you.

 Seventy-three percent of people agree that they *do* want to know about their partner's previous relationships.

---

3. The injustice collector.

On their special weekend package deal at a hotel, the phone rang at seven-thirty in the morning and woke Ginny and Barry up. It was Ginny's friend Alice K. wanting to talk. Later that day, Barry asked Ginny to tell Alice K. not to call that early. Ginny reminded Barry that his friends have called at all times, and she never complained. Once, in 1997, his friend called at one A.M. from jail to borrow bail money and she never complained. Once his friend called when she was in the bathtub, and she tripped getting out to answer the phone and she never complained. Once, when she had a migraine and had finally fallen asleep after seventeen hours of excruciating pain, his friend called, and guess what? She never complained.

Five Signs of an Injustice Collector
- You never forget to cite the time, place, and detailed account of everyone who ever hurt, undervalued, inconvenienced, or humiliated you.

- You have trouble accepting an apology and equal difficulty in apologizing. Forgiveness is confused with an admission of guilt.
- You don't feel warmth and safety within your relationship and show it with complaints and outbursts.
- You feel easily ashamed.
- You are very sensitive to rejection and very verbal about it.

> **NOTE:** Shame develops for a variety of reasons. It could be a brother in jail (something outside of you), a physical feature (something on you), or an unacceptable thought (something in you) that releases feelings of shame in a person.

 What a Line
Ed, a fisherman, surprised his girlfriend by taking her fishing and tying the engagement ring to her pole. Then he handed the pole to her and waited till she noticed. She spied the ring dangling in the sea. She said yes.

What to Do If You Can Chronicle All Your Hurts Before Your Joys

Ask yourself:

- While the events may be real, are you sure your interpretation of them is correct?
- If not, what would that mean? How would you then feel?
- What does injustice collecting do for you? For the relationship?
- Have there been times when you were able to fight back against the urge to be an injustice collector? How did you do it?

- How could your partner comfort you when you start injustice collecting?

What to Do If This Is Your Partner

- Give credit for your partner's tolerance of injustices whenever credit is due to her, and even beyond. Give extra credit.
- Cultivate her sense of humor. Make up credit coupons, credit dances (cha-chas, ballets, Native American dances). Call forth the credit gods and make sure she knows they are on her side.
- Know that when she starts her injustice collecting lecture, it's because she feels rejected, a break in the connection to the warmth. Help her find it again by not taking up where she left off and continuing with more of the problem. Stop yourself when she cannot stop herself.
- If she brings up previous injustices or feelings of shame or rejection, listen carefully and take her worries seriously. Don't dismiss them. Don't tell her they aren't true. *Just be there to listen!*
- When she starts in, give her a hug and say you're sorry.

> NOTE: Never underestimate the power of saying you're sorry, even when you think you didn't do anything wrong. Saying you're sorry is never a defeat. The courage to end an argument, to take the high road, is always a victory.

The Good News

The good news is that you have many more resources today for managing your insecure feelings than you had when you were two. The mission, should you choose to accept it, is to reevaluate behaviors that do not encourage a deepening of intimacy, and thus, do not help you feel more secure. It takes courage to let go of anything, whether it's an extra ten pounds, the pileup in your closet, or the insecurities of a lifetime. Here are some good reasons to keep at it.

1. When you make positive changes in your style, the relationship becomes more satisfying.

Face it. The things you were doing when you felt you weren't getting enough reassurance did not work to help you get more. You ended up feeling worse about your partner and yourself. In fact, sometimes you broke up over these things. It's time to try another way.

2. You can put an end to the feelings of being undervalued and unwanted.

Even if you have felt all your life that people were short-changing you and not meeting your needs, when you rethink how you've reacted and handled that, you start noticing more positive feedback from others—feedback that may have always been there but that you haven't noticed. Whenever you seek reassurance in more positive, direct ways you can be proud of yourself.

3. You can learn to need less attention and thus be more satisfied in your relationship.

When you are less needy, you stop pushing people away.

4. Adopting new behavior styles will help your future spouse be more loving.

When you learn to need less attention by developing a support circle for yourself and by changing your reactions to your partner, you make room for your partner to offer you more of her own free will rather than because she feels overwhelmed with your neediness. Your partner can be more loving.

Don't get discouraged. It'll be easier than this.
Thomas Edison struggled for years to invent the
lightbulb. He tried over 999 times before he finally
got it right. After he discovered how to channel
electricity, he was asked during an interview how it
felt to have failed at it for so many years. His reply
was, "I don't consider that failure. I learned nine
hundred ninety-nine ways not to do it."

5. You'll feel so much better about yourself.

When you give up old roles that had you acting critical,
bossy, clingy, you start to realize that those roles weren't really
you. You are a reasonable person, a lovable person, and you can
be loved just for being yourself rather than demanding love.

Well, you've got some suggestions for how to manage the
need for reassurance and the fear of being let down. As you re-
view them, it will be so-o-o-o-o easy to spot pieces of your
partners here. I did. You may even find yourself fuming because
you are reminded of something that's happened in the past or is
happening currently. Resist the temptation to focus only on
your partner. This chapter will be most helpful when you locate
parts of yourself, too.

So ask yourself the following question every day:

What is it like for someone to be in a relationship with me?

Answer it honestly.
Then do something about it.

Are You a Poll Taker?

Mitch asks his friend Eric how many times a week Eric and Irene have sex, how long foreplay lasts, how many fights they have per week, and how many times they talk on the phone to each other on a normal day. Then he calls Mandy and Lois and asks them. Then he reports back to his girlfriend, Carol. He tells her that they fight about twenty-five percent of the time, while Eric says that he and Irene get along ninety-five percent of the time. Mandy and Lois get along eighty percent of the time. Mitch tells Carol that they are not doing as well as their friends.

Mitch cannot trust himself to make a decision or express a feeling without taking a poll. Without people to tell him how they feel, he has no idea how he should feel. Polling puts him in touch with medians because he is uncomfortable with feelings. Mitch is so afraid of criticism that he uses polling to reduce emotional contact with others. He substitutes information for real feelings of affection and attachment. Polling masks his feelings of helplessness.

If this is familiar to you, ask yourself:

How do you feel when you make a decision?

What would happen if you made a wrong decision?

What is the price to pay for making a bad decision?

What do you imagine people will say if you screw up?

What do you think about when you consider trusting yourself?

How do you feel when people criticize you?

Has there ever been a time when you made a decision you felt good about? What was happening to help you to do it?

Hey, trust yourself. Life will be easier when you do.

You Overrate Marriage

Many people aren't married yet not because they think so little of marriage but because they think so highly of it. Do you seek a whammy that will have you vibrating the way Mickey Mouse vibrates when Minnie Mouse strolls by? Do you long to remain endlessly enthralled with each other's moles, minute mood shifts, earlobes—the forever feeling that, out of all others in the world, you have come upon the one who is perfect for you? Not like your last lover who you *thought* was perfect until you knew him better, or the one before that who tried to fool you into *thinking* he was perfect. No, this lover *is* perfect.

Isn't it great to find yourself "lost in his arms" or "swept away" to the point where you can't even remember your ATM number? Isn't it sweet to melt as you take two hearts and make them beat as one? What a nice rest!!

This stage of love is important in the development of a relationship because it allows us to reexperience total *trust*, that first and long-gone feeling that if you cry, Mother will hold you . . . if you need, she will be there.

That whammy isn't given up easily. No wonder we give it up kicking and screaming. Those who can't let go of it and move forward to the other stages of a relationship are easy targets for making major mistakes about love—mistakes that will lead to unfathomable disappointments. Here are three of the most common mistakes of falling in love with love—mistakes that mean that you won't be able to massage that love into a happy marriage.

 Meet My Better Half

The idea of two hearts beating as one is older than you think. Plato wrote about merging two people to create one whole person when he described a man alone as having only one side, like a "flat fish." Plato came up with the phrases "your better half," "your missing half" as he searched for his.

Don't get the idea that this is a he/she thing. Plato's missing half was not Plata, but another Plato.

Mistake 1: Love erases hurt.

Each one of us has a deep, inner pain that is enclosed in an emotional safe. It hurts like hell, and we'd do anything to get rid of it. It's always there. It doesn't leak, it doesn't move, it doesn't give. It's kind of like a breast implant, but instead it's a pain implant. The pain results from all the things we fear will happen to us, all the things that have happened to us, all the things we fear we are, all the love we didn't get. It is there when we go to sleep, and it is there when we put our pants on in the morning. It is there when we are on vacation, and it is there when we put our nose to the grindstone. We are on intimate terms with this pain. We would do anything to shed it. Some of us try with drink or food or prayer or plastic surgery or simple denial. At best, we find temporary relief. Then one day you see this man ... he smiles at you ... you avert your eyes ... you smile back ... your heart thumps wildly ... his heart thumps back ... and, for the first time in your life, nothing can hurt you, all psychic pain is gone. You wait a while because you want to be sure. And then, you're sure. It's gone, gone, gone. On one hand, you are shocked, and on the other hand, it is exactly what you expected.

Of course, you must have him. All of your energies go to that. And then you dream of what it would be like to be together. And then you are together. In the beginning, you are happy beyond reason. But, as novelty gives way to knowledge, it hits you with all the force of an Evander Holyfield right hook: Life still hurts. The pain is still there.

Though each person's pain is as unique as a fingerprint, it also contains universal themes such as:

- pain of not feeling like you are important enough
- pain of not feeling lovable
- pain of feeling passed over
- pain of not feeling wanted
- pain of past hurts
- pain of feeling that things won't improve no matter what you do

Some of us think so highly of love that we believe that when we find the right person, all of this hurt will dissolve forever. The right person can dissolve our hurts—*temporarily*—during the idealization phase of love.

Real relief from pain comes when you discover that your most painful beliefs about yourself (I'm unlovable, I'm second best, I'm inadequate) are just that—beliefs that were never true. Call me a red monkey devil, but life and love are not as easy as we've been told and not as easy as we'd hoped.

Mistake 2: Being in love feels like falling in love.

Twelve-year-olds fall in love, but we don't let them marry because marriage is not for children. Being in love is not for children either. In fact, the longest and potentially richest stage of your relationship, the "being" in love stage, is founded on a loss—the loss of the enveloping passions of falling in love. Many couples never make it from one stage to the next.

I know this story firsthand. At one point in my life I felt with utter certainty that love had died because it was my rotten luck to choose the wrong men. In truth, I knew how to *fall* in love, but that was about it. I constructed a labyrinth of ways to repeat falling in love with the same person over and over again—all of which included living on an emotional roller coaster to keep it sexy and new. As soon as I approached a deeper phase of commitment, I panicked. I fought. I left. I did anything I could do to create enough drama to shake myself back into the familiar stage of falling in love. Falling in love was the only way I knew how to keep a relationship going. When I'd exhausted all aspects of it, I quit.

I developed a habit of not dating anyone who lived closer than fifty miles to me. On the surface, it seemed that this policy was a way of slowing the relationship down and protecting myself from making a mistake. The truth was that, with a minimum of fifty miles of distance, I could keep the honeymoon, the falling in love phase, for longer periods of time. I set it up so we just couldn't see each other frequently enough or long enough to get past it. When I met my husband, he lived 215 miles away from me. This was perfect because, since we could only see each other once or twice a month, I could maintain a continual level of intensity. I did so for over a year. Because the intensity had been maintained for so long, I believed it would last forever, so I moved to New York to be with him. Although I did not understand what was happening to me, when I no longer had distance as a way to regulate the falling in love stage, I panicked. Without consciously knowing what I was doing, I replaced "distance" with "fighting." I started fights so we could break up and then get back together again. Within two weeks of moving to be with Boots, I initiated a pattern of chronic fighting. I did this over and over again over a span of years. I followed a relentless configuration of being certain I'd made a mistake, breaking up, missing him, getting back together. I used breaking up to regulate my emotional state and keep it at a "beginner's" level. I was stuck in the falling in love stage of the relationship. In fact, I know now that I'd never gotten further than that in any romantic relationship in my life. Nobody bothered to tell me that one day love is no longer just a feeling, it becomes a point of decision. How come they didn't teach this stuff in school? How come I spent a whole semester in Home Ec learning how to sew an apron?

 In 1727, British satirist Jonathan Swift wrote a poem about a shattered love affair:

> And yet, I dare confide in you;
> So take my Secret, and adieu.
> No wonder how I lost my wits,
> Oh! Caelia, Caelia, Caelia shits.

Yes, we can feel shocked to discover that our loved one is flesh and bone and what she ate for breakfast.

My problem was that I did not know how to make the transition between falling in love, which is a state of being fused, and being in love, which entails a recognition of differences. Making this transition involves a decision to give up the treasured fantasy of love as the easy union of two soul mates.

In my work with single adults, people are always wondering if they are with the person they should marry. Recently two clients were discussing that matter. They both had partners whom they thought they loved, but there were things about them they did not love. One night, they both started asking me what to do. I never tell anyone what to do, but I did tell them that they were *exactly in the right place*. At some point, you see all the possibilities of the relationship and all the problems of the relationship and you *decide* to *be* with that person even though you won't always *feel* like being with them.

Can't Live If Livin' Is Without You
There are people who feel that their love is tied to their survival. When you meet someone who says he feels totally unsafe in a relationship, who spouts words such as, "I can't live without her," he is saying that love and survival are entwined. What he means is that he is still caught in the symbiotic phase of love that Plato talked about where we are searching for our missing half. If you can't live without her, it's because she supplied the other half of you. Without her, you're half a person and half a person can't survive.

Mistake 3: Never go to bed angry.

You're not going to like this. It will go against everything you've been taught about relationships (although, if you're anything like the rest of us you've been taught more about how to floss your teeth than about love). What I have to tell you is something that I've been saying for years and years in individual, group, and couples therapy. The people I've said it to didn't like it either . . . at first. In fact, my publishing house wouldn't let me put it in my last book because they said my position on it was too strong, and that it would be too unpopular. I don't want to be unpopular. But what I have to tell you can save your relationship and, someday, it might just save your marriage. So, even if you *hate* what I'm about to tell you, and even if it makes me unpopular, I'm not doing my job if I just ignore this message. Furthermore, you will probably thank me for it someday.

The most important thing about marriage that I've ever learned has been the hardest and the most difficult to accept:

A long, happy relationship that includes the freedom to feel love cannot exist without an equal freedom to feel hate.

No one can bear to talk about this. No one told me. No one wants to think it might be true. People speak of love, honor, commitment, tenderness, goodwill, empathy. The word *hate* never gets mentioned. We read that love heals emotional hurts. That's true, but not before it pushes the button of every emotional agony you've ever had, intensifying them a million times. Every single person who comes into my office believes that love is going to make them feel better about themselves—that if they could find good love, all wounds would be cured. Love. A welcome flood of sweet nectar. We *love* that feeling. But hate? We *hate* that feeling. At best, it makes us feel like jerks for thinking we ever loved this person. At worst, it makes us behave in terrible ways.

The truth about true love is that most divorces could be avoided if couples understood

- as much about their bad feelings for each other as they did about their good feelings for each other
- that it's as natural to hate your partner as it is to love her
- that when you have hateful feelings it rarely means the love has died
- that hate is nothing to be afraid of or to run from
- that the less scared we get when we feel hate for our partner, the better the love can be
- that the more we accept our hateful feelings, the less we feel the need to act on them in negative ways

You see, the problem is not hate, and it never has been. The problem is the way people act when they feel that emotion and the way it makes them feel about themselves after they've given hate the upper hand.

Marriage is a feeling gym. It is a place where you work out all your emotional muscles. The key is to learn *how to act toward your partner* when you don't feel loving. Meanwhile, it's fine to kiss your sweetie good-night after a fight because you have the knowledge that, whatever the fight was about, you'll work it out. It is not, however, fine to shove conflicts under the sheets as if they don't exist simply because it's midnight. That's a fantasy. Instead, get a good night's rest because you'll need it in the morning to resolve the conflict and enjoy making up tenderly, lovingly.

Love Blunders

You Should Make Me Feel Good About Myself

Rene, a saleswoman, has spent six months fruitlessly wooing an account. Suddenly, one day out of the blue, they call her and give her a large order. She calls Ralph at the office to tell him she's made reservations at The Tiki Hut, their favorite restaurant to celebrate. Ralph says he has a lot on his mind, and he's not up to celebrating. Rene asks him if he could put his worries aside for the evening. At this point, he tells her that he doesn't think he can, and he asks Rene to wait a few days until he feels better about things. She slams down the phone, appalled at his selfishness. In the next moment, she feels one of her major migraines coming on. In the moment after that, a new patch of psoriasis rises around her collar.

The blunder: You should make me feel good about myself.

The good intention: It feels wonderful when you offer me praise, validation, and support.

The flaw: If you are going through something and you can't give me support when I need it, I'll be depressed, anxious, and angry. I may even get sick or create a crisis to get attention. It's your job as my partner to meet my needs no matter what you are going through at the time.

The step toward the aisle: Sometimes you won't be there for me, and I'll have to do things for myself. These things are inevitable. I will feel disappointed when you can't be there for me, but I won't turn it into a weapon against you or me. I'll explore my needs without blaming them on your lack of caring. And, okay, I plan to pout.

Love Blunders
You Should Know What I'm Thinking

Adam and Lila were at a party that was boring Adam to tears. After four boring conversations with four boring people, Adam put on his coat and carried Lila's coat over to her. Lila looked at Adam in surprise and said, "I'm not ready to leave yet." Adam replied, "This party is a drag. Let's go somewhere else." Lila said, "It's not a drag to me." Adam answered, "You're not going to tell me you like these people. That's ridiculous."

The blunder: You should know what I'm thinking, and you should agree.

The good intention: We are tuned in to each other in extraordinary ways. That gives us a private world of our own, a way to have private time together even if we are standing in a crowd of people.

The flaw: If you and I can be exactly the same, we won't have to ever be unsure when we are separated from each other because we will know we are part of each other. There's comfort in the idea that we think the same and we can read each other's minds. (Except, it isn't true.)

The step toward the aisle: Although we agree on many things, we're both complex so we also disagree about many matters. It is inevitable that we will disagree on small and important matters. So I won't assume what you are thinking. I'll ask.

CHAPTER 8

You Pick Impossible Relationships

Most of us have been entangled in an impossible relationship (or two or three) during our quest to find a lifetime mate. It takes time and wisdom to know what we need to be happy, not to mention how to make another happy. Most of us learn from our mistakes. Then we make new ones. Then we find a partner and make even more mistakes. We marry and make even more and more mistakes. And we live happily ever after—more or less.

Yet, some of us don't seem to learn. Instead of making *new* mistakes (which I call progress) we can't seem to avoid making the *same* mistakes over and over again. This chapter is for those of you who repeat the same mistakes, the kind that chronically land you in relationships that flop.

Four Impossible Relationships

1. S/he's not a decent person.

Patty met Ray at a party. He's adorable, especially wearing his T-shirt that read, "Here comes a bad boy." The back of his T-shirt read, "There goes a bad boy." He's so energetic— especially after one of his frequent trips to the men's room. And what stories he tells—bicoastal late-night dinners where he entertains his famous clients (which is why you can only call him on his cell phone), a business partner who walked out on him in the middle of a huge deal (and that's why he has a cash flow problem), a sick friend in another state (and that's why he can't make plans for the weekend).

Patty falls for men who aren't decent people, even though she has strong instincts right off the bat that they won't do. What about you? Do you attract men who don't fit in with your friends, whom your parents loathe, who have fatal flaws you can't tolerate—yet, in spite of the little voice in your head, you get deeply involved? Do you just hope the problems will pass?

This quiz will tell you more.

1. You are at an elegant restaurant. The sommelier brings the wine list. Your partner says,
   a. *"Thanks. Do you have a recommendation?"*
   b. *"We'll have a bottle of the Poolee Foosee."*
   c. *"I brought a flask in my jacket pocket, so get lost."*
2. You bring your partner home to meet your folks and she says,
   a. *"I'm so glad to meet you. Jake speaks so highly of you both."*
   b. *"Jake still sucks his thumb. What did you do to him as a child that has him so messed up?"*
   c. *"Oh, Mr. Jones, Jake is so hot in bed. I've learned that when the son is hot, the father is even hotter."*
3. You are lying in bed reading the paper and your partner says,
   a. *"So much bad news. I'm glad we've got each other."*
   b. *"Hey, wanna rob a liquor store?"*
   c. *"Death and destruction is such a turn-on. Will you read to me about this murder out loud while we make love?"*

If you answered three a's, call a Justice of the Peace. If you answered three b's, call a cab. If you answered three c's, call *America's Most Wanted.*

A forbidden, tactless, dangerous partner gives you a chance

to buck your parents like you did when you were a teenager. Or maybe you never even take him to meet your parents. That is even more teenage-like because you are, at thirty-two, still sneaking around behind their backs.

If this mirrors your usual choices, then a stable, interested partner is probably boring and undesirable to you. It would be like, ugggggghhhhhh, having sex with your father. *And, my dear, that's the point.* Somehow you got stuck in the time of your life where you would usually work that emotional crisis out. For whatever reason, you didn't get the help you needed with that— the help that would allow you to stop having to buck your adolescence by having a serious case of bad boy–itis.

Chronic bad boy–itis has its roots in low self-esteem and stunted adolescence—it's the old "I'm not worthy" joke from *Saturday Night Live*. It's a good reason to get a little individual therapy and then go into group therapy. Don't miss out on the good stuff in life. You don't have to remain stuck. I urge you to get to work on this so you can enjoy your relationships more.

2. You are drawn to rivalrous triangles—wanting most what you can't have.

When we are puberty bound, we notice couples walking down the street, kissing against a car, holding hands, gazing into each other's eyes. We know, even at thirteen, that we want to be one of those couples one day. As we grow older, if we haven't found a lover yet, we can start to feel enraged when we see those couples pressing ham against a car. How dare they? Don't they know we're alone and thirty?

Two feelings can be stimulated (among the thousands of other feelings that don't apply to this chapter). The first is desire: You want what they have so you go out and find a man of your own. Now you can be the one to annoy single, lonely people. The other feeling is envy. You want what they have and you are going to get it by splitting the couple up and getting him for yourself. You feel stimulated by the thought of winning him away from her.

If you are always wondering if you are the best lover he's had, if you ask over and over, yet never believe his answer, then triangulating love may be something you want to explore about yourself, so you can work through it and enjoy your relationships more fully.

The envious wish to steal him away can be stimulated by the drive of rivalry and competition. *You* have to be the prettier, sexier lover, and love is tied to winning in a fashion that puts you on top. Or, the wish to steal him away can be stimulated by a belief that you are only turned on by someone who already has someone else. That's the only thing that really makes you hot.

There is yet a third psychological pull into a triangle. Some of us feel so scared of being one on one with another, so unused to or frightened of the full force of intimacy, that we insert another person into the relationship as a mode of self-protection. We fall in love with someone who is married or living with someone, or we have a lover on the side or are involved with someone who does.

Many of us maintain this triangular pattern, and it is this that causes our two or our three broken hearts before we pass through this stage and find a lover of our own. However, if you find that you have been through this more than twice or that you have entered your thirties and are still hung up on people who aren't available, then it is time to get some romantic tutoring so that you can enjoy a one on one, rewarding, intimate relationship. In short, if you don't outgrow this soon, go to therapy and work it out. Don't end up as the other woman.

3. You repeat rotten relationships.

You started the relationship with only the intention of loving and being loved. You made your needs known early on—but not too early. You were kind, considerate, fun, sexy. And now, you are on a *Guinness Book of World Records* version of the emo-

tional roller coaster of bad will, bad sex, bad fights. What went wrong? This has happened too many times for you to keep saying, "It's just my luck."

This is the case where all of your relationships seem to devolve into painful, excruciating nightmares even though you are both nice people who have searched for love in all the right places. The two of you, who cared so deeply at the start, have begun to bring out the worst in each other day after day after day.

If this is you, then chances are that you are undereducated about how to be in a relationship and, believe me, you're not alone. Basically, we've been taught more about how to change a tire than about how to understand what happens in a relationship. So it makes sense that when the relationship hits a rocky reef, you may not have learned how to either steer around it, or steer through it without damaging the boat.

 "I don't know which is a bigger challenge, marriage or music. But they both have their ups and downs."

—Bonnie Raitt

The most common reason for repeating bad relationship habits is that you didn't have a good model to observe as you grew up. That doesn't mean your parents didn't love each other or had a horrible relationship. It can simply mean that they had an agreement about certain ways of relating that helped them maintain their marital arrangement.

Agreements such as:

we don't air bad feelings

we disagree about everything and the one who yells loudest wins

we suffer out loud

we suffer in silence

one always gets his way, the other always submits

we sit on anger until we explode

one of us complains, one of us withdraws

These don't seem to be arrangements you'd want, but, somehow, thousands of us make them and live our lives that way anyway.

If you are wondering whether you've picked up some pathetic relationship habits that mar your ability to feel warm and fuzzy enough to propose, you can take your current problems with your partner back one generation and ask yourself how your parents would have handled the kinds of problems you are having now.

When my parents were unhappy with something

they threatened to leave
they withdrew from each other
they would work it out
they would take it out on me
I rarely saw my parents disagree

My parents' communication style was

loving
civil
contemptuous
threatening
distant

My parents argued about

the same things over and over
different things all the time
everything they discussed
little
I never knew what they argued about

My parents were able to resolve differences

> during a conversation
> within hours
> they stayed resentful
> they stopped speaking
> they yelled at the kids

My parents fought

> rarely
> sometimes
> frequently
> all the time

My parents' arguments seemed

> mild
> reasonable
> intense
> greatly overblown

Rate the following statements from 1 (the least) to 10 (highest rating).

5___ My parents respected each other.
9___ My parents cooperated around important matters.
1___ My parents communicated in a positive fashion.
2___ My parents were not bound by gender stereotypes.
1___ My parents felt their relationship was fair.
1___ My parents worked at their relationship.
1___ My parents showed affection for each other.

Acknowledging the roots of your relationship style will help you:

- feel on more solid emotional ground
- increase your empathy for your partner
- to see your relationship through a more realistic lens
- isolate your issues and develop a plan to resolve them

- understand yourself and your partner better
- behave in less provocative, more mindful ways
- like yourself better, thus making you a better partner
- survive the difficult times without devaluing your partner

Now you can explore new relationship skills that will help you understand the important tasks necessary for a healthy relationship.

4. You don't really want to get married.

Your mother is whining for grandchildren, all your friends your age have married and are having children, everyone you work with is married, your two younger siblings are married, the kid you baby-sat for down the street has announced her engagement. You feel like you are the only single person left. There must be something wrong with you. Does your life go like this:

a. You wake up on a gorgeous day, but all you can think about is *"I'm not married."*

b. You win the lottery, but all you can think about is *"I'm not married."*

c. You have involving work, fulfilling hobbies, and still, when the day is over, you climb into bed obsessed with the thought, *"I'm not married."*

d. You have interesting relationships, both long and short term, but when it comes right down to it, you can't imagine coming home to any of them every night.

e. Your apartment is exactly the way you like it, the leftovers you put in the refrigerator are still there when you wake up in the morning, you take great vacations, you are comfortable in most ways, yet you find your mantra remains, *"I'm not married."*

f. You go on "maintenance dates" with dull oafs as well as nicer oafs, but none of them seems as interesting to you

as your pals, and you'd rather be home reading a great novel or gabbing with a good bud.

Why not entertain the idea that as hard as the culture pushes you, as hard as your unimaginative, misguided relatives push you, you don't really see yourself married? You're having fun with your friends and your lovers and you like doing your own laundry.

Being single never has to mean being alone. You may want to consider rethinking love as something that doesn't need to have anything to do with marriage and instead focus on:

- setting your family straight about the fact that you are an adult who has chosen to remain single
- maintaining and deepening your long-term friendships
- taking on a cousin, niece, or nephew that needs an extra parent
- taking responsibility for your financial future
- enjoying your life to the fullest

You can remain single and have a pleasurable, compelling life. You can have serially monogamous romances or steady dates with other single friends. One recent study of divorced women over forty-five says that these women would never want to remarry and feel that they are much healthier and happier taking care of themselves.

Debunking a Love Myth

Myth: True love is unconditional.

The half truth in the myth: True love allows for shortcomings, small and big mistakes, even a royal screwup from time to time. You and your partner can fail at loving each other without the threat that love will be withdrawn.

The danger in the myth: You start believing in sentiments such as "I want unconditional love, I want to be loved for who I am, not what I do." You back yourself into a corner where you either do or accept the unacceptable and win by unanimous decision the uncoveted title of "Doormat of the Decade."

The reality in the myth: As adults, we need to be responsible partners who love each other for and are loved for our kindness, caring, good deeds, nurturing, etc. You are what you do.

What you can learn from this myth: Only an infant should be able to piss all over you and expect to be loved.

9

You Have Social Anxiety

Did you know that ninety-eight percent of our genetic material overlaps with that of the chimpanzee? Still, you've probably never watched a wildlife special where the chimps are agitated because they've made a social faux pas. With chimps, the mating game is simple, brutal. One male services all the females using the very unflirtatious tactics of domination and aggression. Yes, it's in that little two percent of our brain, that small portion that is "not-chimp," that we possess the ability to compose a symphony, raise a barn, and plan a wedding for 125 people. In the ninety-eight percent lies our vital biological instructions to mate. In the two percent lies the part of us that wants to do it in a more civilized fashion than a chimp—without belligerence, without lice, and without the public scratching of our scrotums.

 "Of course he's your son, he looks just like you."
Animal researchers believe that as many as half of all chimps may be conceived in secret rendezvous where the female chimp sneaks off to mate secretly with a male from a rival gang.

For some of us, that two percent also includes the internal tornado called social anxiety. Social anxiety is what Mark Leary and Robin Kowalski, two academics who write books on the subject, call "the stage fright of everyday life." I'm sure you've known the palm-sweating, stuttering, tongue-tied, stomach-churning, crazy-thinking, adrenaline-pumping, gland swimming, nerve wracking–ness that can come over you when you most want to appear cool. Social anxiety is interpersonal, thus it happens between you and others. There are other kinds of anxiety that occur between you and others, such as when you bring back an overdue library book to a mean librarian or when you think you are being observed by a shifty stranger. It's easy to understand apprehension over such things. But how can we explain the deep dread we can feel before or during a social situation where there are no real threats to our being? How can we explain that we'd almost prefer facing the mean librarian over going to a party with twenty-five nice people?

 Social anxiety is a negative emotional experience that evokes fear of psychological or physical harm, increased nervousness, and the strong urge to escape or avoid the situation that is causing the apprehension. Social anxiety affects thinking, feelings, body language, and the psychology of the person experiencing it. You can feel all this and others may never even know it.

Social anxiety varies in intensity and duration, and the kind we are talking about occurs around situations such as those illustrated by the following:

Center-of-attention anxiety: Lacy was out with Beau and Bernie, the twins who just moved in down the block. "Boy, are they cute," Lacy was thinking, as the twins recounted all kinds of twin-pranks they'd played. Lacy was laughing out loud, and she could see that they were both interested in her. It was all going so smoothly, when Beau and Bernie simultaneously said, "So, tell us about yourself?" As the attention shifted to Lacy, she became aware that all eyes were on her, and she froze.

Attractive-people anxiety: Chelsea is a firecracker raconteur; the life of the party, she can make conversation with any man she's *not remotely interested in*. When the cute guys head her way, she's paralyzed.

Heterosexual anxiety: Georgia can make a new girlfriend in a millisecond. But when a man starts to talk to her, she's so nervous that she can't even understand what he's saying, much less connect.

Body gland/noise/size/shape anxiety: Irving is sure he's too old, too fat, and too sweaty to find love, even though no one's ever complained about his looks. Then there's the issue of his penis, although with Viagra, the sky is the limit. But, forget it. He's sure if he could ever get that far, he'd fart in bed, and she'd run for cover.

Asking-for-a-date anxiety: Quentin can discuss the theory of relativity and/or *90210* with equal conviction. No problem. But, when he tries to ask Valerie out for a date, his mouth feels like he's just been bitten by a puff adder.

Foot-in-mouth anxiety: "Anyway, what's the most egregious thing you could say?" Helena asks herself as she sits with Greg. Calming herself, she decides to tell him she's so glad he called. She opens her mouth, and "I'm so glad you're bald" comes out.

Tripping-on-a-banana-peel anxiety: Manny knows he'll fall down on the way into the restaurant, or, better yet, fall onto a waiter about to serve duck flambé. That's all he can think about, even as Rachel's doe eyes gaze at him warmly.

Yes, social anxiety hits when you have an increased desire to make a good impression, alongside a decreased belief in your ability to convey the impression you want. We've all paid a visit to the heebie jeebies, caused by the real or imagined shoddy evaluations and judgments being made about us by the people we meet.

The Evolutionary Roots of Social Anxiety

To understand the roots of social anxiety, I sought consul from my dog Sparky Jones because, as a pack animal, he represents the most basic issues in an easily understandable way.

1. We're pack animals.

Like Sparky, we're pack animals and our deepest need is the need to belong. We want to be with other people, even when there is no apparent advantage to it. Like Sparky, we are gregarious. We are loyal. We hate to end relationships, even bad ones. Alone, we feel lonely, rejected, vulnerable. Thus, social anxiety encourages us to act in ways we hope will fulfill our need to be part of the pack. It keeps us from hitting, hurting, biting others. It keeps us searching for acceptable behaviors that will have us included rather than sent to the doghouse.

 Myth: Anxiety ruins my social life.
Truth: Your relationship to your anxiety is the real problem.
Suppose you treated your anxiety like a needy friend who needs to talk to you? You listen with compassion, but don't let his problem take over your life. Try learning to be on better terms with your anxiety. That time will be better spent in working toward having that good relationship with anxiety than in wishing the anxiety would disappear. Try being gentle with it, and see what happens.

---

2. We're hierarchical.

Like Sparky, we organize with the dominant on top, the submissive on the bottom. Submissive doesn't mean "weak." Sometimes the sweetest of us are the ones who lie down on their backs for a tummy scratch while more dominant ones enter punching. Dominant people, like dominant dogs, control the resources. They maintain dominance through a series of facial expressions, vocal cues, and subtle manipulations that signal acceptance or displeasure. Sparky is not so subtle—he humps. We, the submissives, negotiate to live in the packs alongside the dominant without combat, without conflict, without unwanted humping. Social anxiety tells us when there is tension ahead. It urges us stop what we are doing and check it out. It interrupts our behavior. Thus, social anxiety is part of an evolutionary attempt to get along.

It's Very Clear Our Nerves Are Here to Stay

I wish I could get rid of your social anxiety, but you can see how deep it runs. However, I am sure you didn't buy this book so you could spend years and years trying to eliminate something. No, you want a spouse. I can help you get one anyway. You can get spoused if you will agree to give up the idea of becoming an un-stressed person and settle for being a person who is willing to function even though you feel like a mess inside. Changing your perspective on social anxiety can help you reduce it by twenty to sixty percent.

Try the following tactics, reject them, try something else as you see fit. No one tactic will work for everyone, and no tactic will work all the time.

Tactic 1: Blush and bumble on purpose for at least ten minutes morning and night.

Give up the same old same old that never worked and, instead, do the opposite: Make yourself a wreck. Scrunch up your face. Try to recall a blush, a word salad, a Chevy Chase pratfall. Yes, it's paradoxical. Nonetheless, many people have gained more control over their anxiety by learning how to induce the symptoms at will. This teaches you more about your body, your triggers, and the mechanisms at work. Where in your body does it start? Where does it move? How fast? You don't have to feel helpless and uninformed about your body; you can learn how your nerves work. So, before you go to work, sit at your breakfast table, and make yourself blush. When you come home from work, take ten minutes and do the same. As you learn to do *more of* your problem, you learn to gain more control over it.

 "Be bold and mighty forces will come to your aid."
—Shakespeare

Tactic 2: Walk naked through the locker room of life.

You know how when you don't want to say the word "face-lift" in front of your Aunt Sylvia who just had one, but all you can think of is "face-lift face-lift face-lift face-lift face-lift face-lift"? Well, it's the same thing when you don't want to appear nervous when you are. There is no choice: You will screw up. So, take the pressure off yourself and screw up right off the bat.

 Darwin addressed shyness, embarrassment, and blushing in his writing. He said that shyness was close to fear, but not like fear. For example, a shy man may not like strangers, but he doesn't fear them. He may be a hero in a battle, yet too scared to eat in front of his date.

In the first ten minutes trip over your chair, drop your wallet, and rip your pants when you try to pick it up. Yes, practice your Laurel and Hardy routine because if you humiliate yourself right off the bat, you won't have to ruin your date by wondering when you will. If the two of you can live through the ice cube that fell from your mouth onto the tablecloth, it's a very good sign.

Tactic 3: Give up the constant search for approval.

My friend Jody described her first six dates with a wealthy man. He was arrogant and overbearing and she nonetheless found herself altering her personality to get him to like her. We often spoke of our struggle to act outwardly in a way that is consistent with how we felt on the inside—how to be more authentic. Disappointed in herself, she stammered, "I was such . . . such . . . such an approval suck." We both started laughing because the phrase captured the struggle to a tee—trying to seek approval from boyfriends, bosses, taxi drivers, store clerks, and searching constantly for people who would tell us we're okay (even people we didn't like).

 Myth: It's important to be relaxed.
Truth: Ninety percent of people aren't relaxed.
Research studies show that more than ninety percent of people have experienced social anxiety at some point in their lives. This includes everything from self-described shyness to dating stage fright. When your evil twin whispers "Your anxiety isn't normal," it's probably not true. Almost everyone you've ever talked to—even those whom you've perceived to be calm, cool, and collected, knows exactly how you feel.

Pleasing others (sucking approval from our partners) can be the goal in relationships even when approval can only be achieved at the expense of hiding our own needs. This phenomenon has been called "doubling," a way of developing a functional second self that is imposed over the true self and keeps the true self away. The true self holds the authentic emotions while the second self holds the conciliatory behavior. This was what was demanded of Africans during the tragedy of slavery. African-American poet Paul Laurence Dunbar wrote a poem called "We Wear the Mask" that begins, "We wear the mask that grins and lies." Doubling is similar to "wearing the mask"—you behave the way you think you must behave. Over time the "mask" may systematically erode the real self.

When we meet someone who interests us, we enthusiastically adjust ourselves with only the intention to build love. Make sure you don't end up overdoing it because you'll feel like an approval suck or, as one comedienne (whose name I wish I remembered) described it,

"So I'm sitting across from him in the restaurant, acting exactly like the woman I'm sure he wants me to be—one who has absolutely nothing in common with me, and I'm saying, 'He's perfect.' "

Tactic 4: Brush up on your social skills.

Many people experience social anxiety simply because they have had less training or experience regarding their social skills. Perhaps their parents didn't do much socializing so they aren't used to people coming in and out of their lives. Shyness is understandable. If you are someone who has less experience socializing with others, the good news is that you can do something about it. The best way is to enter an arena where you will see the same people on a weekly basis over a period of time. Some ideas are volunteering to do sets or lights for a community theater, joining a church choir (bring a box of donuts for all), taking up yoga or tai chi—anything that will get you interacting with people.

Tactic 5: Enter group therapy.

If you spend a lot of time worrying what people think about you, then, of all kinds of therapy, group therapy will give you the chance to check out your assumptions about yourself as you gain confidence and give and get feedback, reality testing, and support. Ask around until you find a group that focuses on social relationships. If you have difficulty finding a group, you can find out more about how to do this at the end of the book in the emergency section.

Tactic 6: Decenter yourself.

I hate to be the one to tell you this, but, while you are totally absorbed in how you are coming across, your partner is feeling the same anxiety. While you are sure that your partner can sense your discomfort, she is worrying about the same thing. While you anticipate that she will be turned off, she anticipates that she will turn you off. Meanwhile, no matter what you two think you look like, neither of you is likely to resemble Don Knotts when you are nervous. You can shake inside and most people won't even notice because *they are too busy worrying about how shaky they are.*

Yes, when *you* are nervous, it is hard to think about how everyone else is feeling. Chances are that, without realizing it, you may be so caught up in the idea that you are being judged by others that you don't realize that you aren't giving them a chance. Your partner is just as anxious about how she is coming across. If you overfocus on yourself, you have nothing to give.

It's time to focus on how to help her feel safer. Increase your awareness of your impact on her so you can be conscious of how you push her away by only thinking about yourself. Shyness won't hurt you. In fact, bashful and shy in the right combination is endearing—it's a turn-on. It's only a turn-off when you forget that you are with someone who needs your attention. You know you're shy, but you may have her thinking you are remote and unreachable.

Tactic 7: Make a public service announcement.

If you know that your nerves get in the way of getting closer, then do yourself and him the favor of saying so right up front.

"I get shy in the beginning till I know you better. If I'm quiet, it's probably because I'm nervous, not uninterested."

"So far, although no one has sustained major injury, I've stepped on five toes, spilled six drinks, and fainted two . . . well, make that three times. It's shyness, not you. So let's not dance or drink for a few weeks. As for the fainting, just fan me and sing out loud. I always come to."

"This is a public service announcement from the *fill in your name*-Is-a-Klutz Foundation. This is National 'Have Pity on a Bungler' Week. Take a clumsy man to lunch and be eligible for the grand prize."

Stress-Reduction Tips

1. Think back to times when you successfully handled stress in the past.
2. Identify what part of your body is affected by stress, and then work to relax that part of you. For example, purposely tense up your shoulders. Now relax them and notice the difference between the two feelings. Do the same with other parts of your body.
3. Take a long slow yoga breath through your nose and release it gently through your mouth. Continue to breathe deeply and slowly.
4. Roll your head slowly in a circle.
5. Don't ask yourself "what if."
6. Accept that your anxiety is *natural. Everyone* has it.
7. Shake out your hands every fifteen minutes to half hour.
8. Imagine you are in a warm, safe place.
9. Relax your facial muscles and unclench your jaw.

10. Talk back to your negative thoughts.
11. _____ (This space is for your idea.)

Debunking a Love Myth

Myth: I'm helpless against the feeling of falling in love.

The half truth in the myth: Love is our most powerful force.

The danger in the myth: When you say you are helpless, you are automatically evoking excessive dependency, which leads to a desperately unbalanced match.

The reality in the myth: We got the idea of defenseless human captured by love from the Greeks who revered Eros, the petulant baby god of love. Eros, or Cupid, shot random arrows at unsuspecting souls and then disappeared for his New Year's Eve gig, leaving only his quiver and a few Baby Wipes. The myth of love as a random event stuck, even though we know that love stands its best chance for survival when partners are equal, knowingly taking responsibility for their choices.

What you can learn from this myth: Even a moth, drawn to fierce flame, can decide to fly away unharmed as it feels the dangerous heat. You too can feel an unbelievable pull to be with someone and make the decision not to give in to the urgency.

CHAPTER 10

You're a Snoop

(dedicated to my favorite snoop)

When Daniel leaves early for work on Monday morning, and Marla, who leaves much later, has time alone in his apartment, she looks through his desk drawers. If you asked her why, she'd tell you it's curiosity and maybe a bit of fear that Daniel has things going on that she doesn't know about.

Certainly we get curious about people's private places—a medicine chest, a wallet, a journal, a closet. It can be hard not to take a little peek. What about you? Are you an occasional peeker or an out and out snoop? This quiz will tell you more.

Are You a Snoop?

Rate yourself 1–5 for each question.

1 = never

2 = rarely

3 = sometimes

4 = often

5 = it's chronic

_____ I peek in the medicine chest when I go to someone's house for dinner.

_____ I check to see what prescription drugs people are taking. I want to know who's on Prozac and who's on something else.

_____ I check book jackets to see if they are inscribed by former lovers.

_____ I look in my partner's drawers when he's not home. It's a nervous thing I do when I'm antsy.

_____ I look in my partner's drawers to see what he is keeping from me.

_____ I dust his fly for prints.

Add up your score.

6–13: Consider yourself an Angela Lansbury without her own show—a snoop, but acceptable for family viewing.

14–24: Too much snooping. No matter what you think is going on, you need to take a deeper look.

25–30: Don't skim this chapter! And don't think that this behavior is okay because "everyone does it." Your behavior is bound to bring you more than you've bargained for and less than you've hoped for.

Why Do You Snoop?

When you snoop, you rarely say, "Oh, let's see if he is going to surprise me with concert tickets." Instead, you are looking for something that it will hurt you to find *and that you already know is there*. Intense sensations overload you as you wait for the right moment, open the drawer, and begin to go through it. Then you panic as you forget what was where, hastily repack the drawer, worrying that you'll tip him off. Clearly, something urgent is happening.

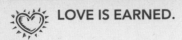 **LOVE IS EARNED.**

The urgent thing inside of you has two parts:

1. You are trying to expose your partner because you are too scared to expose yourself.

When you fall in love, you open your emotional drawers to your partner. You want to expose yourself, but at the same time, it is terrifying. Exposing yourself means sharing your deepest thoughts, weaknesses, feelings, inexplicable idiosyncracies—things that make you feel vulnerable. What if you expose yourself and he leaves you—or worse, betrays you? What if he is shocked, or finds you less lovable? Some of us snoop because, if we can expose our partner, we won't have to risk letting ourselves feel exposed.

 Questions a snoop should ask herself:
What will happen if I find what I'm looking for?
What will happen if I don't?
What is going on in my head right before I snoop, as I'm snooping, and right after?
Will this help love grow?

2. You want to discover the true nature of your partner, and you can't trust yourself to discern it.

Snooping is one way we try to prove the true nature of our partner, so we can decide whether we can take the risk of trusting him. But in looking for your lover's exes, fetishes, and transgressions, you are actually in the business of transgressing. The rationalizations for snooping take many forms, and they illuminate your style within your relationship. How do you disseminate the test of trust? Here are the hypothetical possibilities for what you might be thinking.

Rationalization: You make up a story to justify bad behavior.

I dropped an earring and I thought maybe he found it but forgot to say so. When I looked in the drawer I was looking for my earring.

Denial: You deny reality.

I didn't do it. I would never . . .

Doing and undoing: You think like a kid, believing you can undo what you did by doing something else.

I'll look in his drawer now, and then later I'll make love to him the way he likes it.

Submission: You don't take responsibility. Instead, you claim that you are victim to a force larger than yourself.

I can't help it. Something came over me. I looked in the drawer.

Avoidance: You keep yourself on the run so you don't have to think about the drawer.

I'll take my aerobics class. I'll make lunch. I'll study for my test. I won't think about it.

Aggression: You think you are entitled, and you use aggression to make your point.

I'll look in his damn drawer. I have every right to do so.

Which one is you? I'll bet that this isn't the only place where you employ this style. It is likely to be evident in many other situations in your future and your past. Think of the ways you fight, work, and make your way through the day. Chances are that your character style can be understood the same way your snooping can be understood.

Are You Looking for a Way In or a Way Out?

Everyone keeps a secret. Everyone has something they don't want you to see, or to know about. And in the deepest most abiding love—where there is the most to lose—we will all hold on to something that could endanger that love: a dirty little picture, a sexy little note. A little piece of us toys with disaster because we are human, because we have a trickster in us, because we thrive on a little dangerous stimulation, because we like to test ourselves, because it gives us an edge, because even in the deepest love we take stupid little risks.

 Two Thumbs Up

Hollywood has earned millions with the age-old formula of one partner hiding something from another. In the movie *Sorry, Wrong Number* Barbara Stanwyck's snooping uncovers her husband's plot to murder her. In *Midnight Lace* Doris Day discovers her handsome Rex Harrison wants to do her in. In *Spellbound* Ingrid Bergman tries to discover the true nature of the man she is falling in love with, Gregory Peck. Is he a murderer or just a tortured man? In *Malice* Bill Pullman discovers that the love of his life (Nicole Kidman) is the scum of the earth. The fear that we have missed the true nature of our love is a provocative theme that captures our dark imagination.

So you have to decide whether you are looking for a way in to a relationship or a way out. If you are looking for a way in, then you better get yourself to the point where you can love him, secrets and all, because a relationship that is organized around a fear of betrayal creates too much anxiety. You'll be too edgy to get any closer than you are right now. Snooping is a way to keep your partner at a distance and then say it's his fault.

Searching a drawer is what you do when you want to toy with the idea of ruining things for yourself.

Proof

As much as each of us wants to be good at intimacy, and despite our own deep need to be intimate, it can elude us. Our perception of others can be that they are not loving, that they can't be trusted, they do not love us—so we don't want to get close. When you look in a drawer, maybe you seek proof that you are lovable. You can only experience others in terms of the way that you experience yourself. If you feel lovable, others will seem more loving. If you feel worth caring for, others will feel caring. If you feel satisfied, others will seem satisfying. If you feel trustworthy, others can be trusted.

But, if you do not feel lovable, you will feel that you are not good at intimacy. It will seem hard to get what you want from others in your relationships. Relationships will exhaust you. Your relatives will feel selfish and unresponsive, your friends will seem too needy or self-serving, your partner will feel all of the above and then some.

So, keep reading. Sit and think about it. The real key to getting married is to begin behaving in ways that make you feel loving toward yourself. This is the best reason not to snoop!

Last Words

So you're still scared he's hiding something. Welcome to the club. The feeling comes from a lifetime of not making emotional ends meet. Don't give in to it. Stop asking if you can trust him, and start asking if you can trust yourself.

Of course, it is possible that you have real reason to suspect your partner of betraying you. If that's true, then reread the section in Chapter 8, "S/he's not a decent person," and act accordingly.

CHAPTER II

You're in Love . . . Except for This One Thing You Hate

You love this mook or mookette. But there's this one little problem with his (or her) looks/behavior/hair/politics/taste/job/fashion sense. If s/he could be just a little

- richer
- thinner
- less critical
- younger or older
- more sophisticated
- quieter when s/he eats, sleeps, etc.
- more interested in what you are interested in
- smarter, as in Howard Gardner, yet prettier, as in Jennifer Lopez, yet passionate about his work as in Stephen Hawking, yet bun-tight as in Angela Bassett, yet talented as John Leguizamo.

Face it. You can't live with it. You wish you could, but you can't. There are better weeks and worse weeks. You even have moments, when the light hits her hair in a certain way, when he turns toward you with that mad twinkle in his eye, moments when you forget about it completely. Then, without warning, the cycle starts over again, and you feel *stuck on this one thing* all over again. Still, you hang in there, and every moment you aren't to-gether is a moment you are planning to break up. And, yet . . .

Even when you feel like a fly trapped on flypaper, you aren't actually stuck. *You're simply moving sideways instead of forward—*like Bill Murray in *Groundhog Day*. The movie was a fable where the ill-fated Bill played a mean-spirited weatherman covering the story of Groundhog Day in a small Pennsylvania town he couldn't stand, filled with people he couldn't stand. He was sucked into a time warp where he was forced to relive this same frustrating February day over and over and over again. As if reliving the same day was not hell, he awoke to Sonny and Cher singing on the radio. As if reliving the same day was not hell, he awoke to Sonny and Cher singing on the radio . . . you get the picture.

What makes the movie a fable is that *each day wasn't the same—it was the same day*. Bill woke up in the same hotel with the same people eating the same breakfast in the same dining room on the same calendar day. He had the same job covering Groundhog Day. However, aside from that, he could use the time in any way he wanted. So he spent it devising methods to seduce his costar, Andie MacDowall, into his hotel bed. He flirted. It didn't work. He lied to get her pity. It didn't work. He pretended to love what she loved. It didn't work. Outrage didn't work. A suicide attempt didn't work. As the day(s) passed, though, Bill got to know the townspeople, made friends, saved a life, and built relationships with people who cared about him. He became a more generous man. Then, one day . . . er . . . the same day, Bill woke up feeling happy. He greeted the same peo-ple in the hotel dining room, talked with new friends on the street, became a kinder, warmer person with more concern for others. That was the day he and Andie ended up sucking each other's elbows in bed because:

He was ready for success only when there was a shift inside of him. This internal shift made room for a new experience.

As Carlton approached his fifties, he gained weight. Laura, who had dated him for four years, felt that his weight signified that he had let himself go. The weight was a constant thorn in her side. What a turn-off! One day, Carlton's secretary, Sally, called Laura and told her that the office was planning Carlton's fiftieth birthday party. Sally wanted to invite Laura. After telling Laura the details, Sally confided that the office women swooned over Carlton. In their eyes, he was like a movie star, a dreamboat, a superstud. Many sighs were sighed when he walked through the room. Because he was so admired, not to mention good to his staff, they had decided to decorate all seven floors of the office with two hundred balloons and masses of streamers—a party for the entire staff of hundreds. Laura sat in silence. She was stunned. It was a shock for her to hear how others thought of a man whom she readily described as an aging, chubby boob.

We have all been in groundhog relationships, and you too may need an internal shift to make love happen.

If He Were More Ambitious I'd Marry Him

Although Tony has a good job with a good pension plan, Linda wants him to be more ambitious. Linda knows that he could be more highly rated in his industry. Her concern is understandable—after all, if they get married and she has a baby, his salary probably won't be adequate. So, she suggests to Tony that he might put together his résumé, and he says he will but he doesn't. So, she hangs a picture of Donald Trump on the refrigerator, but he mistakenly thinks she's sexually interested in Donald Trump and that gives him a good laugh. She leaves biographies of remarkable businessmen by the bedside; she cuts articles out of the *Wall Street Journal* and asks Tony to look at them over dinner. She reminisces about their sex life in the old days and implies that power is an aphrodisiac. Tony stubs his toe and misses an important conference where he might have made contacts. Linda tells Tony that other people have mentioned he's not working up to his potential. Tony has no response. Linda throws her hands up in the air. She pleads with Tony. He sighs and takes a nap.

Linda is stuck because *the definition of the problem is bigger than the problem itself.*

Linda defines the problem as one in which the stubborn Tony obstructs her efforts to help him get ahead—something she is doing for their own good. (It doesn't have to be ambition. Linda could want Tony to be thinner, more outgoing, or any number of other things.) Based on her definition of the problem, Linda puts her heart and soul into helping Tony. She

1. asks
2. teases
3. insists
4. reminisces
5. bristles
6. criticizes
7. pleads

Linda thinks she's working hard. Little does she know that what she is working at is maintaining the status quo. Everything she tries is a mere variation along the continuum of *making Tony change.* Just like Bill Murray trying to make Andie MacDowell change, when one attempt to persuade Tony fails, she escalates to a harsher variation. Does she think that if she hangs on just a little longer, one of her plans might finally work? I mean, put yourself in Tony's shoes. How would you respond? Would you feel helped? Even if you wanted the same thing she wants?

In the old days, a fire horse, the horse that pulled the water and the firefighters to a fire, was walked every day for miles over the same exact route at the same exact time. When the fire horse was retired, when there was no reason to ever walk that route again, the retired fire horse was filled with incredible anxiety if she could not walk the route anyway. In fact, horses died when they were deprived of walking their daily route. We sometimes act like a fire horse in our relationships. We follow a certain trail we know so well we could follow it blindfolded—we follow it, even when it leads us someplace we don't want to go. Thus, we get locked in patterns that keep us stuck.

Linda needs to stop trying to persuade Tony and start thinking more about why she is reacting so strongly to this. Here's a guide for Linda and for you, whether your perception is that your partner is too meek, too chunky, too . . .

Step 1: Explore the position you've taken on any important matter.

Surprise Quiz

Check off as many of the following answers as you like:

I believe that if I

_____ prove the reality of the situation

_____ make a logical explanation

_____ ask her to listen to reason

_____ suffer long enough

_____ yell loud enough

_____ blame

_____ evoke his guilt

_____ get friends to agree with me

_____ get my partner's mother to align with my position

_____ bring up the subject at the right time

_____ withhold sex until I get my way

_____ tie my partner to the sofa till he recants

_____ write to Ann Landers and show it to him

_____ pray

_____ practice voodoo

_____ make a wish to my angels

my partner will see the error of his ways and change.

Stop collecting the negative.

Okay, okay, maybe the voodoo will work. However, in general, if you continue to make him the problem (or even make his problem the problem), you will continue to feel stuck. No one is asking you to like something you don't like, but if you want to feel better, stop asking "How can I get him to do what I want him to do?" Instead,

Step 2: Ask yourself the following questions.

Why does my peace of mind hinge on trying to make him into someone else?

What worries erupt inside me when he doesn't care about the same things I care about?

How do our differences affect the way I see myself?

How does our difference alter the way I see my partner?

Do I think my friends will view me differently if he changes?

And, most important, *What would I be doing with all my time if I weren't so involved in my partner's problem?*

> NOTE: Only move ahead here if you really want to get married. Otherwise, you will be much better off complaining about your dates for a few more years.

Step 3: Give *yourself* a break.

We tend to handle problems with our partners much in the same fashion that we handle interior conflicts within ourselves. This being so: *You will be just about as hard on your partner as you are on yourself.* So when Linda hounds Tony, it's a great way to avoid hounding herself, because hounding Tony takes so much time. And if you are hard on yourself, you will be hard on your partner. If you feel as if nothing you do is good enough, you will feel the same about your partner. Ask yourself:

- How do you handle your internal conflicts?
- Do you agonize over things gone wrong?
- Do you get mad at yourself when you screw up?
- How long do you stay mad at yourself?
- What are the messages you send yourself when you are mad at yourself?
- How do you treat yourself when you are mad at yourself?
- Are you a known perfectionist? A repeat offender?

Only when you are willing to take a step back from your fury, take the focus off what *he* does to you, and take the time to look at what *you* do to you, will you be ready to tackle the first step down the aisle. By the way, if you cut yourself slack, you will cut your partner slack.

Step 4: Know that there will *always* be something you hate.

Shaniqua is a nonentity during the basketball season, and no amount of reasonable whimpering will change that.

Conor's fiancée will only have sex with him if he takes a shower, and he feels that the spontaneity is gone.

Chang's fiancée talks to her mother on the phone every night at eight on the dot.

Jackie's boyfriend is a slob who leaves a trail wherever he goes.

Sara's boyfriend has maxed out his credit cards.

Harry doesn't like his girlfriend's cats.

Kyra wishes her boyfriend brushed his teeth more often.

I said this earlier. It bears repeating:

A long, happy relationship that includes the freedom to feel love cannot exist without an equal freedom to feel hate.

Recently I made an appearance on *Oprah* to discuss the subject of "Lightning Fast Love." The audience included a front row of couples who fell in love at first sight and married within months or even days. These couples had never had a fight—not even one teeny-weeny altercation. They agreed on everything, including child rearing, sex, money.

Whenever a couple comes in to see me for therapy, I always ask in the first session how they met. Couples who jointly tell the story, who smile at the differences in their recollections, who each tell half as if they've told the story many times before, are the couples who stand the best chance of making it. Most couples, even in the heat of hurt, can somehow get back to the good feeling of their initial meeting.

My comment was that, if this were true, they ought to have the decency not to tell us about it. Because the only three couples in the world who felt this way were going to make the rest of us want to kill them.

The reality is I have rarely met a happy couple who didn't have one major thing about their relationship or their partner that they couldn't stand. It can be a behavior, a physical feature, a relative. Don't kid yourself. It's okay to have something you just can't stand.

Step 5: Find the perfect future in the present.

I have a favorite short story about relationships that I give to many of my clients to read. It was written more than 100 years ago by Nathaniel Hawthorne, and it is entitled "The Birthmark." I never cease to be amazed at Hawthorne's perspective on life and love. In the story, a brilliant scientist has a wonderful, loving, beautiful wife who has one flaw he hates—a red birthmark on her cheek. As much as he loves her, he can't turn his mind away from the birthmark, and he devotes his science to creating a potion to eradicate it. His happy wife didn't even notice her birthmark until he began to point it out. As he kept bringing it up, she began to hate it, too. She was willing to do whatever he wanted to get rid of this blight on their pure love. He tried many potions that did not work, increasing his frustration and his commitment to finding the one that would allow her perfection to shine. Eventually he created a perfect potion and asked her to drink it. She did and fell into a deep sleep. And, as he watched, the birthmark faded before his eyes. But then, his wife awoke and told him that he had "rejected the best the earth could offer." And with that, she died.

So, even though there is one thing you hate, I hope that you will not fling away an attainable and happy future for an unattainable perfect present. Marry the best that earth has to offer. And, by the way, Happy Groundhog Day.

Assessing Yourself

Your fantasy of the feelings you will have when you fall in love tells you what you need to focus on within yourself.

- If you fell in love to get comfort then you need to learn about comforting yourself.
- If you fell in love to get attention, then you have not learned how to attend to yourself.
- If you fell in love to get approval, then you need to work on your self-esteem.
- If you fell in love to find happiness, then you need to find what makes you happy.
- If you fell in love so someone would be there, then you need to explore your own fears of being alone.
- If you fell in love so someone would take care of you, then you need to learn better ways to take care of yourself.

Love Blunders

We Should Want the Same Things

Arthur dreamed of owning a cottage at the beach. When he was almost ready to propose to Suzette, he came to her and told her that he had a wonderful surprise. He was sure she'd be as happy about it as he was. He'd made an offer for a house by the shore instead of renting the place they'd rented for the last two years. Suzette balked. She told him that she didn't have much interest in taking on the responsibility of a home, especially one that would be a prime target for salt damage, dampness, and hurricanes. Two weeks at the beach were more than enough for her. Arthur was hurt. This house had been his childhood dream, what he had been working toward. It felt like a physical blow to discover that Suzette had no interest in it—maybe he shouldn't propose to her as he had planned to do the first night at the beach house.

The blunder: You should want what I want. As individuals we are incomplete, together we are whole.

The good intention: The belief that we are part *of* each other gives us the courage we need to commit.

The flaw: No healthy person can consistently match our own internal experiences. Unless you are prepared for this, you may experience a feeling of being duped, as in, "We don't have the same values. How could I have ever thought this was the person I loved?"

The step toward the aisle: I can't expect what is good for me to automatically be good for you. As separate individuals, our relationship represents our commitment to work on ourselves through interacting with each other in a relationship. For my part, I will recognize your individuality, and be mindful of our partnership. However, I'll keep needling you about the beach house, but I'll call it what it is: coercion.

You're a Late Bloomer

Some of us like to wait until we are older to get married. We have other priorities. However, some of us wanted to hook up with a mate long ago, yet we didn't. Instead of thinking something is wrong with you, consider that you may be a late bloomer. For good reasons, now is the right time and then was the wrong time. People bloom later for all sorts of reasons, such as these:

- You are in recovery from substance abuse or you grew up in a home where there was substance abuse.
- There was a family divorce or death at a critical time in your development.
- You are in the process of overcoming shyness and/or anxiety and/or depression.
- Your parents' relationship with each other was so cold and troubled that you must work for a long time on understanding that relationships can have much promise.
- You or a family member had a chronic illness that interfered with building a relationship.
- You had a lengthy, demanding education followed by a demanding job, all of which slowed down your social development.

- You are young at heart in many ways so you felt too young to be in a relationship, even though others of your chronological age saw it differently.

I, myself, was a late bloomer who married the first time far too early for me to sustain a relationship. The marriage I'm in now started more than twenty years after my first marriage ended—at just the right time for me. I had a troubled childhood that included bouts of adolescent depression. Romance comics and romance movies were my life raft. I remember sitting in the kitchen with my mother when she said, "One day it won't be like this anymore. Someone will love you, and take care of you, and everything will work out." Of course, she meant well, and I hung on to those words and leapt at the first man who proposed to me, not thinking at all about much besides what dress I'd wear. So, if you've had the good sense I lacked in my twenties, bully for you.

Tortured with Advice

Valerie made her visit home for Thanksgiving, and as the weekend wore down she sighed a huge internal sigh of relief. For once, the family discussion had not alighted on her marital status, something that always left her totally depressed. Her sister offered to take her to the train station. When they got in the car, her sister led off with, "You keep picking the wrong men, you know." The conversation devolved from there and Valerie found she spent the next day at work crying. Finally, her secretary had to bring her tea bags to put over her eyes.

The hardest part of being a late bloomer comes in dealing with the busybodies who torture you all along the way. In my practice, I am constantly amazed with the stories I hear about "well-meaning" parents, siblings, friends, and even total strangers who, upon hearing you aren't married, offer:

Surprised disbelief: I can't believe it. You're so cute, sweet, you have a great job. There is no reason on earth that I can think of why you haven't been scooped up.

Advice: You're too picky. You need to visualize him, his height, what he does for a living. You pick the wrong people. You don't look hard enough. You look too hard.

Guilt trips: I'm your mother/father/sister/aunt/best friend and I'm not going to be around forever, and I need grandchildren/nieces/godchildren. Sylvia Bernstein down the street is only fifty-two and she has seventeen grandchildren.

Actually, this is no laughing matter. These kinds of comments make late bloomers feel as if they are concealing some terrible, shameful secret that makes them unwantable. This is not true. Don't listen to these "well meaning" people around you. *In subtle yet no less hurtful ways, they are suggesting that something is wrong with you.* Don't accept that they are well meaning for a minute. They are at best uninformed, at worst hostile. They have no empathy for you, no matter how much they tell you they want to help.

So, I've come up with a few responses for the next time someone asks you why you aren't married yet.

- I'm a late bloomer.
- That's a great question. What do you think?
- Because I get scared I'll end up with someone like you.
- I am married. My significant other is doing life in Sing Sing for axing someone who asked me a personal question.
- Excuse me, I don't think I heard you right. I thought you asked me why I'm not married yet, but I know you have more class than that.

You don't need to make any excuses for yourself. I want you to refuse to be tortured by others. Lastly, I want to give you the good news: There are lots of other late bloomers out there.

You're definitely not the only one. Some, like me, didn't know we were late bloomers so we have previous marriages under our belt. And some, like you, have the good sense to wait until they are ready.

 With the help of a Velcro collar, Tabitha Soren and Michael Lewis honored their cocker spaniel, Vegas, as their ring bearer at their wedding.

PART III

Postcommitment Stress Disorder

You've gotten your own drawer, snooped through her drawers, window-shopped, and—er—proposed.

Now what?

CHAPTER 13

Where Do We Go from Here?

Postcommitment Stress Disorder

Oh my God!
I'm in a relationship.
Am I ready for this?
Am I too young?
Too set in my ways?
What am I doing?
What if I find out something really really horrible about this person?

 In African weddings, a bitter herb is used to symbolize the growing pains of marriage. Pepper is used to symbolize the reconciliation between the families.

Every couple is different. The nuances of their intimate communication, their baby talk, their tugs of war, their sexual pleasures, their late-night conversations are unique to them. As you grow into each other, you will find your own "couple personality." It will show up in the way you enjoy your similarities and in the way you express your differences. Did you know that couples who argue frequently stand just as good a chance as couples who never fight? In fact, studies have shown that couples can shout their way through life, rarely agreeing on anything, and be happier than couples who never raise their voices and seem quite agreeable. It's not the fighting that matters so much as the discipline not to be mean. Healthy disagreements of all kinds are to be expected. Amazingly, discussions in which you were sure your partner would put up a fight can go smooth as punch, while the seemingly insignificant decisions can trigger World War III. That's why it doesn't make sense to compare yourself to other couples when you try to understand your relationship. It's better to compare yourself to different phases within this relationship you're in now.

Meanwhile, you do need a game plan for handling situations that could create conflict in the future. In my experience as a marriage counselor, there are certain red flags that all couples can expect to face—facts of life, so to speak. I think my game plan is simple. I think two basset hounds could manage it. So I could be embarrassed to admit that it took me twenty-three years to get it. But I'm not. Better late than never, I pass it on to you:

> *Never assume anything about how your partner was, is, or will be.*
> *Never assume your partner thought what you think he thought, is thinking what you think he's thinking, will think what you think he will think.*
> *Never assume anything about child-rearing roles. If you want to understand your partner's position, thoughts, and feelings, raise the subject and ask directly.*
> *Never assume she or he will feel the same way when the time comes.*

 Margaret Mead said, "Marriage is a long conversation."

This being said, the two of you might want to begin discussion about certain topics. I say *begin* because these are subjects about which people's feelings change over the course of a life.

Topics That Will Be Important in Any Marriage

The two of you ought to have a general sense of how you feel about these matters.

1. Friends and family (your entire MCI calling circle).

When you stand at the altar, you will be facing each other, and it will feel as if you are the only two people who exist in the universe. But, when you walk back down that aisle after the ceremony, you will get a gander at all the others who will be part of your life. So, start talking.

 Boots is a musician. When we got married, I assumed he would tell me when he took a job that required travel, especially international, extended travel. I was shocked the first time I asked him if we could have brunch that Sunday and he told me we couldn't because he was leaving for Japan. It just never occurred to him that he should notify me. It never occurred to me that he wouldn't. *Never assume anything— no matter how obvious it seems to you.*

Do you foresee any changes in your relationship with your friends and family when you get married?

What would they be and how would they happen?

How much time do you want to spend with your friends and family?

How will you decide whom to spend holidays with?

How can the two of you handle intrusive friends and family members so that it doesn't put a wedge between you?

What should the two of you do if you can't stand having dinner with his best friend?

What's too early to take phone calls and what's too late?

2. Socializing.

How do the two of you feel about socializing?

Are your socializing needs fairly equal?

If not, how will that be handled so one partner doesn't feel as if he's missing out while the other feels as if she's being dragged along?

What should the two of you do if you want to stay longer at a party than he does?

What kind of money do you think you should be spending on vacations and entertainment?

Do you tend to be late or early? How will you handle differing styles?

3. Money.

There is no single right way to handle money in a relationship. As long as the two of you are comfortable with it, it's fine, no matter what anyone else thinks. However, feelings about money change over a lifetime, so you might want to note:

What are your present feelings about money?

How important is it to you?

What kind of spender are you?

Do you both plan to work—even after having kids?

What scares you about money?

How will the two of you handle bills?

Will you pool, split, have one joint account and individual
accounts as well?

How should you decide?

Should you discuss important purchases together prior to
making them? Why or why not?

Are you in debt? How much? How do you manage debt?

Will you be renting or buying, and how will that be handled?

While there is no right way to handle money between two
people, couples sure fight over it, so why not try to understand
more about your partner's plans and positions about how the
two of you will go deeper and deeper into debt together.

4. Housework.

The two of you will be running a household, if you aren't
doing that already. There are bills to be paid, trash to be trashed,
tires to be rotated. If the two of you have a style that you are
both comfortable with, skip this section. Don't start trouble
where there isn't any. But if you've been doing the laundry and
you aren't sure you want to be the only one doing it, if you have
certain ideas about who should do what, then read on.

First, let me say housework sucks. It never ends. No one likes
it. Oh sure, you might relax when you polish the car, but there's
so many other things that need to be done regularly. So why not
take inventory on how the two of you operate your homes.
Then, you may want to follow this plan to make things feel reasonable: *Document what needs to get done and set up a schedule.*

I pay my entire credit card bill at once. Boots *always* has a big balance. I never dreamed that he would handle money in such a different fashion. At first, he scared me, and I scared him. It's taken us years to even begin to fathom each other's financial style, let alone agree. But we rarely argue over money anymore. After all, we have found so many new things to argue over.

Take a few weeks to make up a list of all household tasks and the frequency with which you think they ought to be done. This is important because she may put down "dishes" and think they should be done once a week. Taking a few weeks is important because you are bound to forget things you do (or don't do). Then pour a tall lemonade, sit down together with that list, and take a look. Figure out how long the tasks take.

NOTE: Frequently there are contributions we make such as repairing of the car, walking the dog, recycling newspapers, that go unnoticed.

Note the things you both hate doing and the things you like doing. Then decide how the two of you want to handle what needs to be done. Come up with a plan for running the house and a plan for what to say to your partner when you notice she's not pulling her weight.

 Boots has very specific needs regarding the proper placement of dish towels. Since he is dish man, I try very hard to live up to his expectations in this matter. I was leaving them in the sink where they constantly got soaking wet. This was a matter on which he stood firm.

5. Children.

Couples can fall in love and marry without ever having said a word about children. Oh, they tend to know if they want them or not, but often everything else is assumed. Here's a guide to what you ought to have some sense of:

Do you want children?

How many?

What are your thoughts about when to start a family?

What lengths would you go to to have a family if you don't get pregnant?

What are your ideas about a religious upbringing?

Public school or private?

Can you agree on names for a child?

Who's getting up in the middle of the night?

Do you want the baby to sleep with you?

What are your ideas about disciplining a child?

What's important to you about children?

What are your thoughts and feelings about your own childhood—what do you want to do the same and what do you want to do differently?

 Boots and I had been together for six years when we sought some premarital counseling. The counselor asked us about whether we were going to have children. We were dumbstruck. Although it did not seem possible, we had been together all those years without that subject ever coming up.

---

6. Doubt.

As you prepare for the very serious step of getting married, it is natural for both you and your partner to have moments of doubt. Doubts about your dreamboat are natural, no matter how solid your relationship may feel. Doubts don't need to be tied to an upsetting event. They can begin as an intrusive concern that seems to come from nowhere or an apprehension that nags like a tickle in your throat. The shifts in feeling knock against your moods like a bumper car, demanding attention. You'll be asking yourself, "Can I live with *that*?"

 The ringing of wedding bells after the ceremony was meant to scare away evil spirits that would destroy the couple's happiness.

Understanding doubt starts with understanding falling in love. When you fall in love you should bask in it. No one should miss out on the preposterous notions of our partner's perfection. But, after we've learned what that feeling is like, it's time to move on to all the other feelings a relationship evokes.

The truth is that, given that your partner is a decent sort, second thoughts signal that you've decided to make your relationship even more meaningful in your life. You are as willing to explore what makes her hard to love as you are to enjoy what makes her easy to love.

Your partner doesn't need to know all about this, although it's fine to talk about cold feet. However, giving her a lengthy treatise on the things about her that make you uncertain is just a way to shake her confidence in the relationship. A good marriage depends just as much on knowing when to keep your mouth shut as it does on knowing how to say what you have to say.

7. Sexual plans.

Yippee. The two of you are going to have seventy-five years of hot sex together. That should give you just about enough time to get it right. Don't forget to turn each other on by talking about all the things you want to do to each other. If you start getting comfortable talking about sex now, the sky is the limit for what you can expect in the future, because you will be able to experiment with all kinds of different things done in different ways. It's fun to talk about sex—to say what you want and what you want to know, to express your fantasies and desires and hear all about his. Here are suggestions:

I WANT:

to be held

to slow down so I can savor every moment

your head between my leg

to masturbate while you watch

to use a vibrator while you masturbate

to talk about sex

help with learning to be more direct about my needs

you to tell me in detail what you like most

you to let me try things and tell me while I'm trying what feels best

you to show me with your own hand

to know what I do that you'd like more of

to know what you thought was our best sexual encounter for you and what made it best

you to tell me how I can make it easier for you to ask me or show me what you want

to learn the best ways to please you with my hands, my
   mouth, my penis

you to tell me what I do that takes away from you being hot

to know if there are things you want me to stop doing

to know what you'd like me to do longer or harder

you to know how much it excites me when I'm exciting you

you to touch my _____

to narrate sex when we have it

8. Think in threes.

Remember in the movies when Bogart or Gable or Lana or
Joan said something like, "It's bigger than both of us." Well, in a
mature love, this is true. It's essential that you look at yourself
and your partner as part of something that is bigger than either
of you individually. *You must think of your relationship as a third
being—like your infant—that the two of you have committed to love,
honor, respect, and protect just as you have committed to love, honor,
respect, and protect each other.*

 Change your posture within the relationship from
the "I" to the "we," from the individual position
to the couples position, from "his" problems to
"our" problems.

Cupid is a baby, and that's no coincidence. The honeymoon is
the infancy of your relationship. Just as any infant, it needs care,
nurturing, love, and attention so that it can thrive. In order for
love to thrive, you must change your thinking within the relationship from "I" to "we." Thus, when you are making decisions,
think in terms of three:

What's good for me?

What's good for him?

What's good for the relationship?

For example, you are talking on the phone when your partner comes home from work, and you are enjoying your conversation. It might be good for you to keep talking to your friend. Your partner might not care that you are on the phone because he might want a glass of soda, and he might be focused on that. But what's good for the relationship is that you *hang up*. The relationship could thrive if you give your partner the respect of knowing that he or she is more important than gabbing with a friend.

On a grander scale, you get offered a huge salary increase, but you must relocate. Your partner just started a new job, and he doesn't want to move. It's good for you to take the job. It's good for him to stay put. But, when you start thinking about what is good for the relationship, a whole new set of considerations appear: you'd be able to buy a home and start a family sooner; you'd be able to get out of debt; after you'd settled in, you'd have more time together and better health care. Based on these added bonuses for the relationship, it might be best if you take the job.

Thinking in threes means you:

- honor your relationship every day whether you feel like it or not
- invent ways to solve problems
- are willing to make mistakes but retain your vision of your love
- are flexible enough to change direction at any point
- tinker till you find the right formula for your love
- enjoy peaks and tolerate valleys
- know when you two need a vacation
- remain open to new ideas and new ways of doing
- recognize that there is rarely one right way

- hold fast to your love when others have long ago given up on theirs and moved on

---

 The most romantic present Heather Locklear received from her husband, Richie Sambora, was a handcrafted box made out of guitars so she could have a place to hold all the love letters he'd written to her.

Conclusion

As you two talk about the above topics, you might want to add a discussion of wedding plans. Do you want just family and close friends or everyone you've ever known? Are you inviting ex-boyfriends? Children under ten? Cousins you can't stand? Are your folks divorced so you have to think about where to sit whom? What ideas do you have for your first dance? Will you wear white? And, the date . . . isn't it time to pick one?

PART IV

So You're Going to Get Married

The Most Important Things You Will Ever Learn About a Great Marriage

What fun to celebrate your love. You couldn't have picked a better time for a wedding because, these days, we know more and more about what makes marriages work and how to help couples find real satisfaction in a long life together. Researchers have actually found patterns happy couples use, although unknowingly. I've written about them in different places in the book, and you will find more of them in this final chapter.

 The New Bubbly
Studies show that couples who own hot tubs report happier relationships and less stress. Some are even registering for hot tubs as wedding gifts. After all, you can't fight in a hot tub.

I love to celebrate love, too. I've loved love all my life. When I was eight, there was a series of romance comic books. I started a neighborhood ballet school on my patio (my clients were five-year-olds) so I could earn the money to buy them all. The kids' parents had that hour of peace and quiet they always talked about. I charged a quarter—the cost of one comic book.

Later, I graduated to steamier, stranger, and more repressed love, reading *Gone With the Wind*, *Rebecca*, and *Jane Eyre*. It gave me a hankering for dark, brooding men with a secret. I thought *that* was *romantic*. Years later I discovered *that* was *depression*.

But, this is no time for sadness. It's time to dance and sing and talk about your exciting future together, to cherish all that love has brought you, to think about how best to join your lives. I've learned a lot about joining lives and true love through the years, and I continue to learn in several ways:

1. I observe the couples I treat—what they say, what they do, what they learn, what works, what doesn't work, what they have to overcome, and how they put that into the practice of becoming a happy couple.

 Never walk through the door and yell, "Hi honey, I'm home." Always go and find your partner and give him a proper greeting.

---

2. I observe the couples I know and admire as well as the couples I meet everywhere I go. I'm always curious about what they think makes a marriage work, and I always ask. One man told me his thirty-five-year marriage is happy because his wife, who is definitely the boss, has the grace and good sense to let everyone else think that he is. Another told me his long and happy marriage stayed that way because both he and his wife felt free to admit it when they couldn't stand each other. Yet another told me it was because he knew when to bite his tongue.

3. I think, listen to, and read about love—from Plato to Dorothy Parker to David Buss—hundreds of books on attachment theory, love, anatomy of love, biology of love,

psychology of love, heartbreak, repairing love, finding love; hundreds of novels, written about lovers, by lovers; songs and poems about love from Homer to Cole Porter to Babyface.

4. I reflect on my marriage to Boots, and how I work at that.

I've been with Boots since 1985. Before we got together, I had been married twice. (Boots was never married before me.) I didn't know then what I know now. Perhaps that is why I've devoted my professional life to helping others with their relationships. I made so many mistakes before I got it right, and so many mistakes in my own relationship with Boots, as well. My many mistakes created a strong drive to understand love and loving. And I was lucky enough to learn from the mistakes I've made.

 For every angry deed, studies show you must perform six good deeds to balance out the bad. Couples with a ratio of six good moments for every bad one are much happier.

I want to tell you a bit more about what I know—things I haven't talked about yet—that will prepare you to spend the next hundred years in love with the same person.

1. Your childhood, happy or sad, will not necessarily predict whether your marriage will be happy or sad.

The good news is that people with difficult childhoods don't have to worry as much as they do about having a good marriage, and the bad news is that people with happy childhoods might have to worry a little more about how to have a happy marriage. People who experienced little empathy when they were young will need to learn more about what it feels like, so they can understand how to give and receive loving gestures—to practice empathy and disclosure as described in earlier chapters.

 Engagement rings date back to the ancient Romans. They believed that the roundness of the ring represented eternity. Once, it was even believed that a vein ran directly from the ring finger to the heart.

As to why loving parenting isn't necessarily better preparation for marriage: Many loving parents can't tolerate it when their children feel frustrated, so they bail them out. They bail their kids out of money problems, fights with friends, etc. I have found that a number of people who come from loving families leave their parental homes never having experienced the kind of frustration the rest of us have. They go into relationships with expectations of the same kind of support they got at home, and they are surprised when their lovers don't do what they want or give them what they want or fill their needs in the same way their parents so readily did.

No matter what kind of history you have, you will have to work at staying in love by being open to learning more and more about yourself, your partner, and your relationship.

2. Couples must work toward building tolerance to be calm in the face of frustration.

The important marriage skill not often talked about is the need to increase our tolerance for frustration; to stay calm when things are not going well. It's essential to tolerate the things you can't stand about your partner. If you can't tolerate her flaws, you will be critical and start the kind of fights that erode love. You need to be able to soothe yourself when things aren't going your way so you don't get obsessed with what you see as your partner's faults.

Start by learning to tolerate your partner's hot spots (she's always late, she never picks up her clothes, he is a couch potato, he underappreciates you, she's critical). How can you handle these things without losing your mind? You'd better find out.

There is a good reason to learn to stay calm. When you learn to tolerate more and more frustration, *the things that you hate most about him will become less important.* Really. They will occupy less and less of your valuable time. You will have a broader perspective. Building this tolerance for your partner is essential preparation for having children, who will be even less likely to want what you want when you want it.

3. Be prepared to fall in and out of love with the same person over and over again.

When this book comes out, I'll be close to fifty. I'm telling you this so I won't be tempted to lie about my age. Because I only look twenty-three, you might not think I know enough about love to tell you anything. In fact, I know the truth about love, and I have the guts to talk about it anyway. My husband is five years younger than I am. I love him. I am totally attached to him. He drives me nuts. He forgets to do his chores, and he forgets to buy me all the presents I want. When he goes on tour (he's a musician), I am thrilled the first few days to get my house in order. Then I can't stand it anymore. I'd trade my clean floor and made bed for five minutes in his arms. I annoy him with my chatter. I am bossy and critical, but at least I admit it. He is bossy and critical, and he won't admit it. I neurotically finished my midterms the first week of school. He is a procrastinator. My worst qualities and his worst qualities are the world's worst match. Somewhere in the middle of where we both are is one well-functioning human being whom neither of us has met yet.

We've had terrible fights and healthy disagreements. We've sulked. We've gone days without speaking. We've slept in separate rooms—even when we had a tiny apartment and didn't *have* separate rooms. Once he slept in the bathtub.

You are ready to marry when you can fall out of love and then fall back in love with the same person. You will be repeating this many times throughout your long and happy marriage. Believe me.

We have had months of getting along great. We are terrific on vacations together. We have similar values. We love the same music. I find his sense of humor to be the funniest I've ever known. I love his speaking voice. I love to watch him play with our dogs. He is an honorable man who gets up early to walk our dogs even when he's worked late, but then forgets to take the bag of dog poop out of his coat pocket. He has stopped fights, and I have stopped them. When we make up, we usually shake hands.

 Cecilia flipped for Andy Stein, a violin player in a forties' revival band. She watched him secretly, but never said a word. One night, after he'd completed a dazzling solo, she approached him directly. Her first words were, "I love you, Andy Stein." Without missing a beat, he responded, "I know. And we'll do the whole thing . . . get married, have kids . . . but first, let's have a date."

I have fallen in and out of love with him many times. In the beginning, it scared the bejesus out of me. I thought it meant my marriage was going sour. It was a panicky, scary state for me. Thank God, I did nothing drastic. I now know that when I fall out of love, I will always fall back in love, even if I can't see it in the moment. If I forget, I talk to people who remind me. Now that I know our conflicts will end and our marriage will get better, I am nicer. I rarely blow up. Whatever it is, no matter how heated, we will eventually be able to have a conversation about it, and the problem will pass—or, in the worst case scenario, we will agree to disagree. I don't panic. Neither should you.

 Do you know how your parents proposed? Your grandparents? Isn't it time to ask? My grandfather met my grandmother at his engagement party *to another woman.*

---

4. Focus on what is going right.

Build your marriage by focusing on the strengths you have together rather than by trying to eliminate the weaknesses. All marriages have both. Become an expert on what is already working for the two of you, in how you end fights and make up, on the ways you make each other feel special. Do more of what works. Toast even the smallest positive aspects of what the two of you have together.

Conclusion

Oh, I wish I could come to your wedding. Won't you please send me a photo, at least? I leave you with the phrase I heard at my friends Steve and Leslie's wedding. It's stuck in my mind as one of the truer things said about love:

Marriages are made in heaven, but they are practiced on earth. Congratulations.

P.S. Baby photos are welcome, too.

A Few Thoughts on Planning Your Wedding

1. It's your wedding, not your parents'.
2. It is not about family standards or family pressure. It's about your marriage.
3. It's the day to forget that you hate his sister and your aunt. Give everyone a big hug and be merry.
4. Martha Stewart isn't coming to your wedding. So don't get hung up on etiquette and "shoulds." Just do what's in your heart instead of getting married by the book.
5. Have fun at your own wedding. Many couples forget to eat and dance because they are worried they'll forget to say hello to somebody.

Marriage Preparation Courses

There is a plethora of marriage preparatory classes springing up all over. These are seminars for premarital counseling that cover many of the basic tenants of a good marriage such as how to handle differences and money. These courses are helpful:

for anyone planning a marriage

even if you live together

even if you've been married before

especially if you are blending families

for cultural differences

for all marital concerns and opportunities

for family planning

Marriage preparation professionals are varied in background. They may be educators, clergy, psychotherapists, or married couples. Courses vary, but the goal is to teach you how to live together.

Since it is such a new field, there is no central listing, but if you are interested in learning more, and I hope you are, try asking:

clergy

friends

family psychotherapy institutes

the person performing your wedding ceremony

Why not take advantage of all the information and help you can get?

In Case of Emergency: When and Where to Seek Professional Help

Group Therapy

If you feel isolated, depressed, or unhappy with the state of your relationship; shy, easily embarrassed, continually disappointed and/or disappointing, and unable to find a partner with whom you can maintain a warm, supportive romance, then it may be time to call in a professional. Believe me, it's a better choice than beating your head against the wall. My best recommendation for interpersonal difficulties is to join group therapy. After all, you are born into a group, learn your ABCs in a group, and probably work in a group. You can learn a tremendous amount about yourself such as how you come across to others, how you act with others, how you react, and how you build relationships with other group members. In a psychotherapy group, you can explore your thoughts and feelings toward others and how you interpret their thoughts and feelings toward you. You can get and give support and constructed feedback. Most important, you'll learn that you are not alone in your feelings. **I think it is the best way to learn why you aren't married yet and to do something about it—if that is still what you want.**

NOTE: Group therapy has many advantages, not the least of which is that it costs a third to half of individual therapy.

Finding the Right Group Psychotherapist

It is important to look for a *group* psychotherapist, rather than any other kind of psychotherapist. Otherwise, it is like seeing a podiatrist for a soar throat. You should find out if the person you choose is licensed to practice psychotherapy, has had formal training in group psychotherapy, and is a member of the American Group Psychotherapy Association or one of its affiliates.

Really. You can ask these things. A psychotherapist should not get defensive about his or her credentials. After all, don't you want to know that you are putting your trust in the right place? In addition, pay attention to how you feel in the psychotherapist's presence. After all, chemistry applies to this relationship as it applies to other relationships.

If you want to learn more about group therapy, you can write or call the American Group Psychotherapy Association, Inc. 25 East 21st Street, 6th floor New York, NY 10010; (212) 477-2677.

They have a brochure to answer your questions, as well as a referral service to help you find a group in your zip code.

Couples Therapy

You also need to seek professional help if you have someone in your life, and you know you love each other, but the two of you seem to face numerous problems that prevent you from being happy together. As a couple, you need to seek professional help when:

• One of you keeps postponing the wedding date or threatening to call it off.

- Either partner adopts a pattern of getting physically threatening in word, action, or deed.
- One or both of you is depressed.
- There is too much jealousy.
- One or both of you feels a strong urge to cheat.
- No matter how hard you try, things don't improve.
- You feel that the love is dying and you can't stop it from happening.
- You are avoiding serious problems in the relationship, which are only getting worse.
- There is a relative or third person who is intrusive in your relationship.
- One of you is generally satisfied with how things are between you while the other is continually dissatisfied.
- You know things could be better but the two of you don't seem to be seeing much improvement on your own.

Finding the Right Couples Therapist

The best way to find a good couples therapist is to ask friends or family members for a referral. If they don't know of anyone, ask if they have friends who may have sought couples therapy. When others are helped through therapy, they are often glad to tell you about it, hoping you will also be helped.

When you ask for a referral, you don't have to disclose any details if you don't want to. Simply say that the two of you are looking for someone, and if pressed you can say that you'd prefer not to talk more about it.

When you get a name, ask the referrers why they liked the therapist and how long they went. When you call the therapist say, Lisa and Tom Jones gave me your name. My fiancé and I are interested in couples therapy. May I ask a few questions?

Then:

1. Briefly (two minutes or less) describe your problem and ask if the therapist has experience in your area.

2. Briefly ask about the therapist's experience. Don't give the third degree—just find out if the therapist is licensed to practice and has training in working with couples.
3. Ask the fee. (Later, you can call your insurance company and find out if couples/family therapy is covered.)
4. If the fee is too high for you, ask if the therapist offers a sliding scale. If the therapist does not and you can't afford it, ask the therapist if she can offer a referral to someone who can accommodate your price range.
5. Ask how long the treatment usually lasts.
6. Find out if the therapist has hours available at the time you and your partner can attend.

If you have received a high recommendation for a therapist whose fees are out of your budget range, you ought to seriously consider paying the higher fee—as with everything in life, you pretty much get what you pay for. With a good couples therapist, many to most couples begin to see improvement within three to five sessions.

Also, just because some are good psychotherapists, it doesn't make them a good couples psychotherapists. Find out if the person you see has training in couples/family therapy. Couples therapy is a different skill than individual therapy.

In the first session try and get a sense of:

1. The therapist's view on marriage.

You want a therapist who has a bias toward helping couples work their problems out. A good therapist won't have an investment about whether you work it out—that's up to you—but she or he will work with your hope of staying together.

2. Whether the therapist will set goals with you and will stick with what you want to work on.

If your therapist starts off by wanting to delve deep into your past to solve your present problems, expect to be in for long-term treatment. If that is not what you want, say so. You certainly may need to do some talking about your past, but you want a therapist who can stick with the problems at hand.

3. Does the therapist not take sides and make both of you comfortable?

Both partners need to feel comfortable and to feel that the therapist can see and appreciate both points of view.

4. Avoid a therapist who wants to see you both individually as well as together on an ongoing basis.

Couples therapists are trained in many different ways, and it may be that your couples therapist wants to see both of you alone one time. But beware of a therapist who wants to do this on an ongoing basis and tries to get you into individual and couples therapy at the same time with the same person. This creates more problems than it solves because you'll both be wondering what's being said about you when you aren't there. My belief is that your couples therapist can't be either partner's individual therapist, too. If one of you does need individual therapy, it should be with someone else.

Couples Therapy Referrals

If you can't find a well-trained couples/family therapist, try writing to the American Association for Marriage and Family Therapy. Therapists should have a master's degree and a minimum of two years of supervised work with couples. For a referral in your area, write to AAMFT-Referrals, 1100 17th St. NW, 10th floor, Washington, DC 20036

You can also contact the National Association of Social Workers in Washington, DC, the national organization for clinical social workers, which also offers a national referral service at (800) 638-8799. Say that you are seeking a counselor with expertise in couples' therapy.

If Your Partner Refuses to Go and You Know Your Problems Are Truly Serious

If you are in a relationship with serious problems and your partner won't go to therapy with you, you may need to go to therapy anyway to sort out the relationship. There will be signs that you need to do this in the way problems are handled in the relationship. Instead of discussing problems when you are certain your partner has lied to you or when he gets inappropriately pushy with you, you blow up or you have sex and forget about it. Or you send a love note, or you tell him how much you love him. Or you apologize and take the blame. Or you actually deny to yourself any threatening or conflictual information. Or you think that once you are married, things will improve. Or one of you is a substance abuser.

If any of these apply to you, please seek help from a counselor who can work with you to make important decisions about what to do. You deserve a long and happy union, and, sometimes, in the midst of the worst kinds of trouble, the love will win out and the two of you can still end up together. Don't spend your life holding a crummy relationship together when you can learn the tools to find happiness.

Call Training Institutes, Hospitals, and Colleges

If you can't afford group or couples therapy, check out training institutes, hopitals (some have outpatient mental health clinics), and clinics in your area. Training institutes for psychotherapy offer advanced training for experienced psychotherapists and students. Most have a sliding scale. To get this benefit you may have to be willing to be observed in session by students or to have your sessions videotaped for student training. If you don't mind this you can get good treatment at a low fee since all students have experienced supervisors who closely watch their work. One couple I know that is part of one of these programs is treated, as part of a pilot study, by two of the most revered couples therapists in the entire world. The couple pays peanuts for the treatment. You can generally find institutes by looking in the yellow pages under "psychotherapy" or "mental health" or "social service agencies."

Sex Therapy

If you are seeking sex therapy you may write to the American Association of Sex Educators, Counselors, and Therapists (AASECT), 435 North Michigan Ave., Suite 1717, Chicago, IL. 60611-4067, for a list of certified sex therapists in your area. You must send four dollars with your request.

Individual Therapy

While not all psychotherapists are trained to do group and couples work, most are trained to work with individuals. To find a compatible, individual psychotherapist, modify and follow the above guidelines. It's also an option to work on yourself by yourself.

Last Words

Make the call.

For More Information

Sharyn Wolf maintains a private practice in New York City offering individual, group, and couples psychotherapy. She is also a national workshop leader and lecturer. If you are interested in more information, please write:

Sharyn Wolf, C.S.W.
131 West 11th St., Room 1
New York, NY 10011
(212) 414-1241
e-mail: redwolf@datelynx.com

Come visit her online at www.datelynx.com. Click on the red wolf and see what happens.